SECRETS OF A
PRAYER
WARRIOR

SECRETS OF A
PRAYER
WARRIOR

DEREK PRINCE

Chosen

a division of Baker Publishing Group
Grand Rapids, Michigan

© 2009 by Derek Prince Ministries International

Published by Chosen Books
A division of Baker Publishing Group
P.O. Box 6287, Grand Rapids, MI 49516-6287
www.chosenbooks.com

Second printing, July 2009

Printed in the United States of America

This book was compiled from the extensive archive of Derek Prince's unpublished
materials and edited by the Derek Prince Ministries editorial team.

Library of Congress Cataloging-in-Publication Data
Prince, Derek.
    Secrets of a prayer warrior / Derek Prince.
      p. cm.
    Includes indexes.
    ISBN 978-0-8007-9465-1 (pbk.)
    1. Prayer—Christianity. 2. Prayer—Biblical teaching. I. Title.
BV210.3.P74 2009
248.3'2—dc22   2008051181

CONTENTS

INTRODUCTION

Derek Prince was a prayer warrior.

Certainly, he possessed other gifts and attributes. Best of all, Derek was a prolific Bible teacher, with more than 600 recorded messages, almost 60 books in print, and more than 100 video recordings of his teachings. He was a Bible teacher of tremendous depth.

Derek was also the loving husband (over a 53-year span) to two wives, both of whom preceded him to glory. His first marriage took place for him through remarkable direction from the Lord. He married his first wife, Lydia, in 1945, and immediately became father to her eight adopted daughters. (Their ninth adopted daughter, Jesika, was added to the family while Derek and Lydia were in ministry in Kenya.) The irony of this "immediate family" was that Derek had been raised as an only child in a somewhat privileged British culture, and he was a thirty-year-old bachelor at the time. His marriage to Ruth took place in 1978, three years after Lydia passed away—and came about through equally remarkable guidance from the Lord.

Derek was also a philosopher and brilliant scholar, with academic accolades that could fill a page. Another unique experience for him was his service in a medical unit in the deserts of North Africa in World War II—right after the time in which the Lord apprehended him. Derek spoke many languages fluently. He read his New Testament in the original Greek, and was a Hebrew scholar as well. His knowledge and brilliance spanned a wide spectrum. In many ways, he was a true Renaissance man—although he probably would not have considered that a compliment.

A long list could be compiled of the unique events and achievements of Derek's life and ministry, as well as an equally long list of descriptors for him—such as teacher, author, husband, father, spiritual leader and pioneer in many godly activities. Again, Derek would not be pleased for that list to be attributed to him, because he did not consider his life to be about him. It was about Him. Derek would not have been comfortable with such a listing. Nevertheless, of all the descriptors, one would have to be near the top of any list:

Derek Prince was a prayer warrior.

A pastor told of a lunch he and his wife enjoyed with Derek and Lydia back in the early 1970s. In a very natural way throughout their lunch and conversation, Lydia would occasionally touch Derek's arm and say, "I think we need to pray for Jim and Janice." And they would stop and pray for a few moments. And then a little while later, "I think we need to pray for Frank and Betty." Each time, Derek would stop, join hands with Lydia, pray a simple, direct prayer and then return to the conversation and fellowship. According to that pastor, it was one of the most unusual lunch appointments he and his wife ever experienced—but not in an unpleasant way. Prayer was natural and frequent for Derek and Lydia, and later for Derek and Ruth.

Derek Prince was a prayer warrior.

Defining Terms

The statement begs the question: What exactly is a prayer warrior? The best way to answer that question in a definitive way is to read this book.

The complicating factor as we begin the process of answering this question comes from the current state of prayer in the Church. *Prayer warrior* is a familiar phrase within Christian circles, thrown about in a cavalier way. It is used to describe someone gutsy enough to storm the gates of heaven with petitions and spiritual declarations. As you will see when you read this book, Derek did not hold a cavalier view of what it is to be a "prayer warrior." (A good example of such a cavalier approach might be the statement of a song leader at a meeting some years ago, who said, in a moment of exuberance, "I feel so excited tonight! I feel as though I could charge hell with a bucket of water.") Derek, who in addition to other traits had a wonderful sense of humor, would have laughed with the rest of us at that exclamation. But when it came to the topic of prayer, he was anything but cavalier.

An Astounding Statement

We are belaboring this "cavalier approach" to being a prayer warrior because of something Derek says right at the start of this book. In fact, it may be disturbing to you.

In the opening paragraph of chapter 1, Derek's first shot out of the barrel is a statement that sounds alarmingly flippant and egotistical—even smug. In fact, at first reading it (or hearing it . . . Derek stated it routinely when he taught on prayer), one might react against it. Here is his astonishing statement: "For my part, I love to pray—and what is more, I get what I pray for."

At first glance, that statement sounds patently cavalier. "I get what I pray for." Derek plunges in even deeper with his next promise: "That is just what I am going to teach you—how to pray and get what you pray for." All of it may sound dangerously close to the mindset in some Christian circles where we find the "pump in the coins and out pops the candy bar" prayer mentality. The unpleasant picture that comes to mind is the spoiled child begging, cajoling and even throwing a tantrum until God gives in and grants the request. As some have insultingly said, "The Great Bellhop in the sky."

Unfortunately, those kinds of attitudes and approaches are far too common among Christians today. That is why this book will be so very helpful. In the chapters you are about to read, Derek does not teach us how to have our greedy, selfish prayers answered. He teaches us how to align ourselves with the Lord in attitude and practice in such a way that we pray effectively—and thereby get, not simply what we want, but what God ultimately wants.

Aligning Ourselves with the Lord

This concept is well expressed in Psalm 37:4: "Delight yourself also in the LORD, and He shall give you the desires of your heart." Some in the Christian faith might consider that an open invitation to selfish prayers. Indeed, many have misinterpreted that to mean that God will give us whatever we want—any little desire that comes into our hearts or minds. But a friend of Derek Prince Ministries made an observation that would line up entirely with what Derek teaches in this book. His conclusion was as follows: "By delighting ourselves in the Lord, we align ourselves so closely with His heart and desires that what we end up praying for is precisely what His intention is for us. No more, no less." That is a long way from the spoiled child picture described earlier.

Derek makes it very clear throughout this book that there are conditions to be met, habits to be established and proven keys to success in prayer. When we meet those conditions, we see effectiveness in prayer. The kind of effectiveness Derek saw during his lifetime. Because . . .

Derek Prince was a prayer warrior.

The secrets to his life of prayer are no longer secrets. Derek shares them openly and comprehensively in this book. Actually, like most "secrets" of the Christian faith, they were right out in the open all along—brilliantly self-evident in the Word of God. But in his gifted, inimitable way, Derek draws them out for us and makes them plain. Because . . .

Derek Prince was a prayer warrior.

And through applying the truths in this book, we trust you will become a prayer warrior, too.

The International Publishing Team
of Derek Prince Ministries

1

A KINGDOM OF PRIESTS

[Jesus] has made us a Kingdom of priests for God his Father.

Revelation 1:6, NLT

In this book I will be dealing with one of my favorite topics, the topic of *prayer*. For some people, I suppose, prayer seems like an irksome religious duty. For my part, I love to pray—and what is more, I get what I pray for. That is just what I am going to teach you—how to pray and get what you pray for.

As we come to God in prayer, we need to begin with the understanding that He wants us to do so. Most of us probably need to change our negative and unattractive images of God. I know I did. These pictures often stand between God and us and hinder our prayers.

I remember thinking as a boy growing up at school—and I spent many long and rather weary years in British boarding schools—that God was somewhat like a schoolmaster. I really was not too fond of schoolmasters, but that is how

I envisaged Him—sitting at His desk, in His study at the end of a long corridor. If you ever had to go and see this Schoolmaster, you would kind of tiptoe down the corridor. The floorboards would creak as you stepped on them, giving warning that you were on the way. Then as you knocked at the door, the rather grumpy voice would tell you to come in and probably begin by scolding you for something you had done or had not done.

In order for me to be able to pray effectively, that picture I had of God had to change. I have found that there is a similar picture of God in the minds of many—of somebody who is a rather long way off and does not want to be bothered and is probably going to scold us, and, well, the best thing we can do is stay away from Him if possible.

Now that is not at all the truth about God. When we come to Him, He does not scold us; He welcomes us. If anything He says, "Why have you waited so long?"

What a Welcome!

The Bible gives a beautiful picture of how God welcomes us when we come to Him. It is Jesus' well-known story of the Prodigal Son who had strayed away from home, wasted all his living, gotten himself into real deep trouble and ended up absolutely down-and-out. When this young man came to the end of all his resources, his thought was, *I'd better go back home. Perhaps my father will receive me. I couldn't ask him to take me back as a son, but I could ask him to take me as one of his hired hands.* Now I want you to notice how his father received him.

[The son] got up and went to his father. But while he was still a long way off, his father saw him and was filled with compassion for him; he ran to his son, threw his arms around him and kissed him.

Luke 15:20, NIV

See what a welcome this young man got as soon as he was willing to turn around and go back home? He never had a chance to say "Make me as one of your hired servants," because his father was kissing him and welcoming him back as a child.

That is a beautiful picture of how God receives us. He does not scold us; He does not blame us; He is not stern and distant. He is loving and warm and gracious. James 1:5 tells us that God "gives generously to all without finding fault" (NIV). Keep that in mind as you think about praying. God gives generously. He does not find fault. When we get that picture of God into our thinking, it altogether changes the way we pray.

Jesus came to represent the Father to humanity, and the teaching of Jesus on prayer was as totally positive as any area of His teaching. This is what He said in the Sermon on the Mount:

Ask and it will be given to you; seek and you will find; knock and the door will be opened to you. For everyone who asks receives; he who seeks finds; and to him who knocks, the door will be opened.

Matthew 7:7–8, NIV

Notice those three positive statements. Everyone who asks receives; he who seeks finds; to him who knocks the door will be opened. In Matthew 21:22, Jesus said: "All things you ask in prayer, believing, you will receive" (NASB). Again in Mark 11:24, Jesus said: "Therefore I tell you, whatever you ask for in prayer, believe that you have received it, and it will be yours" (NIV).

What could be more all-embracing than those words? *Everything. Whatever.*

In His closing discourse to His disciples in John's gospel, Jesus again assured us—three times—that God will answer our prayers. Listen to these words:

> Whatever you ask in My name, that will I do, so that the Father may be glorified in the Son. If you ask Me anything in My name, I will do it.
>
> John 14:13–14, NASB

If you ask anything I will do it. How comprehensive!

> If you abide in Me, and My words abide in you, ask whatever you wish, and it will be done for you.
>
> John 15:7, NASB

Ask whatever you wish. How could He say more than that?

> Until now you have asked for nothing in My name; ask and you will receive, so that your joy may be made full.
>
> John 16:24, NASB

Ask, and you will receive. There is a special kind of joy that comes from getting our prayers answered. Jesus wants us to have that joy, so He says, "Ask."

To know that Almighty God, Creator of heaven and earth, the Ruler of the whole universe has His ear open to our personal, individual prayer, that He will do what we ask Him to do, individually, is one of the most exciting experiences anybody can ever have.

That is what Jesus taught not only by word but also by example, and His example continues for us today. Let's see how we can follow Jesus into this realm of prayer.

Jesus' Ongoing Life of Prayer

Isaiah 53 gives that well-known and glorious description of Jesus' atoning work. The closing verse reads like this:

> Therefore I will divide Him a portion with the great, and He shall divide the spoil with the strong, because He poured out His soul unto death, and He was numbered with the transgressors, and He bore the sin of many, and made intercession for the transgressors.
>
> Isaiah 53:12

You will notice that four acts of Jesus are recorded here.

He poured out His soul unto death. Leviticus 17:11 says that "the life [or soul] of the flesh is in the blood." Jesus poured out His soul unto death when He poured out every drop of His blood.

He was numbered with the transgressors. He was crucified with two thieves.

He bore the sin of many. He became the sin offering for us all.

He made intercession for the transgressors. Jesus made the most extreme intercession possible from the cross. He said, "Father, forgive them, for they do not know what they do" (Luke 23:34). He was also saying, "The judgment that is due to them, let it come upon Me." And it did.

But Jesus' life of prayer did not stop with His death and resurrection. In Hebrews we read:

> He [Jesus Christ], because He continues forever, has an unchangeable priesthood [one that never passes from Him to other people]. Therefore [in the light of this priesthood] He is also able to save to the uttermost those who come to God

17

through Him, since He always lives to make intercession for
them.

Hebrews 7:24–25

These verses offer a rather interesting perspective on the
timeline of Jesus' life. He spent thirty years in obscurity in
perfect family life. He spent three and a half years in dramatic
powerful ministry. Now He has spent nearly two thousand
years in intercession! The writer of Hebrews gives us further
insight to this ongoing ministry of Jesus:

> Behind the [second] veil, . . . the forerunner has entered for
> us, even Jesus, having become High Priest forever according
> to the order of Melchizedek. For this Melchizedek, king of
> Salem, [was] priest of the Most High God.

Hebrews 6:19–7:1

When I read these verses I always think in terms of the
Tabernacle of Moses, in which two large curtains or veils
hung. Going beyond the first veil correlates to being united
with Christ in His resurrection. It is here that we have the five
body ministries: apostles, prophets, evangelists, pastors and
teachers. Going behind the second veil into the area known
as "the Holy of Holies" means going beyond resurrection to
ascension. It is here that believers are identified with Jesus in
His ascension—seated with Him on His throne (see Ephesians 2:6). Behind the second veil we begin to discover the
two great and final ministries.

When the writer of Hebrews says that Jesus entered in within
the second veil as a priest after the order of Melchizedek, he
was saying that the heavenly order is the king and the priest.
On earth it is exciting to be an apostle if you happen to
be one—or even a prophet. They are wonderful gifts. But
Scripture holds the promise of a much more exciting level of

ministry. Behind the second veil Jesus is Priest and King. We have the opportunity to share in that ministry as well.

The Ministry of a Priest

Most people understand the function of a king: It is to rule. Our participation in the role of priest is not so well understood. Let's start with the one word that describes the unique ministry of a priest: *sacrifice.* In the book of Hebrews we find many places where this relationship is mentioned. Hebrews 5:1, for instance, says, "Every high priest taken from among men is appointed for men in things pertaining to God, that he may offer both gifts and sacrifices for sins." Hebrews 8:3 says, "Every high priest is appointed to offer both gifts and sacrifices." Priests offer sacrifices. We can also turn that around and say that the only people in the Bible whom God authorized to offer sacrifices to Him were priests. (Two kings, Saul and Uzziah, offered sacrifices, and both of them were judged severely by the Lord because they were not priests.)

We understand from these New Testament Scriptures, then, that no person can approach God with a sacrifice or an offering unless that person is a priest. People in general are not entitled to walk up to God and give a gift, even if that gift is a tithe. They must go through a priest.

On that basis, certain words written by Peter might seem to be a contradiction. He told the early Christians that they were supposed to approach God with sacrificial offerings: "You also, as living stones, are being built up a spiritual house, a holy priesthood, to *offer* up spiritual *sacrifices* acceptable to God" (1 Peter 2:5, emphasis added). The verb clearly is *offer*; the noun clearly is *sacrifice*—two words connected inseparably with being a priest. Most of those early Christians were not priests; neither are most of us—and certainly not Levitical priests. What does this Scripture mean? The answer is again found in the example set forth by Jesus.

A Higher Priesthood

During His days on earth, Jesus was not a Levitical priest. The writer of Hebrews states this quite clearly: "If He were on earth, He would not be a priest, since there are priests who offer the gifts according to the law" (Hebrews 8:4). Jesus did not come from the tribe of Levi. He had, therefore, no right to offer the sacrifices of the Levitical priest.

Jesus had a different kind of priesthood, and that priesthood is described in Hebrews 6–7. Look again at the verses from Hebrews that I quoted a moment ago: "Behind the [second] veil, . . . the forerunner has entered for us, even Jesus, having become High Priest forever according to the order of Melchizedek. For this Melchizedek, king of Salem, [was] priest of the Most High God" (Hebrews 6:19–7:1).

We need not look any further. The name *Melchizedek* in Hebrew means "king of righteousness." His name revealed him as a king, and his position was priest of Salem, meaning *peace*. His is the first priesthood mentioned in the Bible (see Genesis 14:18).

The Levitical priesthood under the Law of Moses was a secondary, inferior priesthood. The permanent, eternal priesthood was that of Melchizedek, which is the order of the priesthood of Jesus.

It is interesting to note that Abraham offered his tithes to Melchizedek. In return, Melchizedek gave Abraham two things: bread and wine. At the Last Supper, when Jesus took the bread and wine and gave them to His disciples, He was saying, in effect, "In these elements you see the priesthood of Melchizedek reinstated in Me." These two practices in the Church—tithing and Communion—are the most ancient ordinances in the priestly service of the Lord.

Since Jesus was a priest, though not a Levitical priest, He offered sacrifices even while He was on earth. When we again turn to Hebrews, we find the sacrifice He offered and how this applies to us. Here the writer quotes Psalm 110: "As He also says in another place: 'You are a priest forever according to the order of Melchizedek'; who, in the days of His flesh . . . offered up prayers and supplications, with vehement cries and tears" (Hebrews 5:6–7).

Those words *You are a priest forever according to the order of Melchizedek* were applied to Jesus. We have, then, the three successive sacrifices of Jesus in His priestly role: First, on earth, He offered prayers and supplications—crying out to God; second, on the cross, He offered Himself; and, third, in heaven, He offers the continuing priestly ministry of intercession.

Following Jesus' Example

This example set by Jesus shows what God wants us to become. These words are found in the book of Revelation: "To him who loves us and has freed us from our sins by his blood, and has made us to be a kingdom and priests to serve his God and Father—to him be glory and power for ever and ever! Amen" (Revelation 1:5–6, NIV).

Through the forgiveness of our sins and the cleansing blood of Jesus, we have become a kingdom and priests. Other translations say "kings and priests" or a "kingdom of priests." However it is worded, we can embrace two of the highest functions ever made available to man. God's destiny and purpose for His people is to be a kingdom of priests.

What does it mean for us experientially to be kings and priests? As kings we are meant to rule in His Kingdom; as priests we are meant to offer sacrifices. But notice the specific connection: a kingdom *and* priests or a kingdom *of* priests. God's people are not one or the other. As people of a kingdom it is our responsibility to rule the world for God. Only when we learn to minister as priests can we do this.

What kind of spiritual sacrifices does God expect us to offer? Just as Jesus offered up prayers and petitions during His life on earth, so should we. When we learn to pray, then we are qualified to rule.

Is God Calling You?

Some years ago I became an American citizen. I became one by choice. Believe me, I weighed that decision very carefully. And even though I could see the tremendous possibility of divine judgment falling on America, I decided that I wanted to identify myself with this nation for better or for worse.

Choosing to understand the power of prayer and take your place as a person of prayer in God's Kingdom is no less momentous. Think about it. Are you willing to say this: "God, if You can make me into a priest for Your Kingdom, I'm willing to pay the price"?

Let me tell you there is no higher calling. When you pray, you have reached the throne. Others may not see you because you will be out of sight beyond the second veil, but your life will count for God for time and eternity.

You may not consider yourself to be a strong person of prayer now, but if you offer yourself, God will fashion you. It probably means some changes in the way you have done things, but the difference will be answered prayer. It is not hard; it is very practical. We will learn in this book how to approach God, complying with the basic conditions for answered prayer. We will learn about many kinds of prayer, such as petition and command. We will understand the place of spiritual warfare. We will learn how to know God's will and pray it back to Him. It is possible to pray with confidence. Remember, *God wants us to pray and get what we pray for.*

My prayer for you is that God will bless you in this calling, that He will keep His hand upon you and that He will lead you in paths of discipline and instruction. May He make you what you have offered to be.

Ready? Let's go.

2

BASIC CONDITIONS
FOR ANSWERED PRAYER

He shall call upon Me, and I will answer him.

Psalm 91:15

Prayer is one of the greatest opportunities, one of the greatest privileges and one of the greatest ministries available to all Christians. I do not read that Jesus ever actually taught His disciples how to preach, but He did teach them how to pray. I believe that everyone who seeks to be a disciple of Jesus Christ—who desires to take his or her place in God's Kingdom of priests—should seek to learn how to pray effectively. Remember, God not only welcomes us in prayer, He is waiting for us to pray.

Here, then, are eight conditions that Scripture gives us for approaching God in prayer in a way that will bring answers. These are basic requirements, the first step in getting our prayers answered.

1. Come with Reverent Submission

Hebrews 5:7, as we have seen, speaks about Jesus' life on earth and how He prayed: "During the days of Jesus' life on earth, he offered up prayers and petitions with loud cries and tears to the one who could save him from death, and he was heard because of his reverent submission" (NIV). We studied the first part of this verse from the viewpoint of Jesus as our example of a priest, and how during His earthly life Jesus offered up prayers and petitions to the Father. But at the end of this verse we are told something else that is important. We are told why God the Father always heard the prayers of His Son. It says that Jesus was heard because of His reverent submission. This is the first condition for approaching God.

How was this reverent submission of Jesus expressed? In this verse the writer of Hebrews is referring to the time when Jesus was praying in the Garden of Gethsemane. Here is a description of that event from the book of Matthew:

> And He went a little beyond them, and fell on His face and prayed, saying, "My Father, if it is possible, let this cup pass from Me; yet not as I will, but as You will." . . . He went away again a second time and prayed, saying, "My Father, if this cannot pass away unless I drink it, Your will be done."
>
> Matthew 26:39, 42, NASB

Reverent submission, therefore, consists of saying to the Father, "Not as I will, but as You will. Your will be done." It consists of renouncing our own will and embracing the will of God.

Jesus gave us a prayer to use as a pattern; it is, of course, what we call the Lord's Prayer. In part of this prayer He included this very principle. He taught us to pray: "Your

Kingdom come. Your will be done on earth as it is in heaven" (see Matthew 6:9–10).

When we come to God we have to say, "Your will be done." And within those words resides this meaning: "If Your will and my will are not in accord, then I renounce my will in order that Your will may be done." Where the two wills conflict, it is the will of God that must be allowed to have free course.

There is an aspect of the "old nature" that is being dealt with by this requirement. In his letter to the Ephesians, Paul explained it this way:

> You were taught, with regard to your former way of life, to put off your old self, which is being corrupted by its deceitful desires; to be made new in the attitude of your minds; and to put on the new self, created to be like God in true righteousness and holiness.
>
> Ephesians 4:22–24, NIV

There are two "selfs": The old self is our nature before God changed us; the new self is what God wants to make of us. For the new self to express itself, we have to first put off the old self. That is something we have to do—it is not something that God does for us. So when we say, "Not my will," we are putting off the old self. And when we say, "Your will be done," then we are putting on the new self. That is how we are changed or made new in the attitude of our minds.

If God were to answer all the prayers of the old self in every one of us, the universe would be in chaos. Let me give you just one simple example. The Sunday school children are planning a picnic and are praying, "Lord, keep the rain away." Meanwhile the poor farmer's crops are withering and he is praying, "Lord, please send rain. We need rain." How is God going to answer both those prayers? The truth is, of course, that He is not committed to answer either unless it is the prayer of the new self, which has renounced its own will.

Or take another typical kind of example. Two nations are at war with one another. The Christians in each nation are praying, "God, give our nation the victory." How can God possibly do that? But you see, God isn't committed to do that. God is committed to answer the prayers of the new self, but He is not committed to cater to that old rebel, the old self who just keeps asserting his or her own will.

So when we pray for anything, we need to begin by asking ourselves, *Am I praying for this thing because I want it, or because God wants it?* It makes a great deal of difference. If it is because I want it, my prayers may not be answered; but if it is because God wants it, then my prayers will be answered.

There are certain areas where people habitually bring their requests and petitions to God, such as asking to be healed of sickness or for a financial need to be met. Even in instances like these that we think are surely within the will of God, we still must ask ourselves, *Am I praying for healing because I want to be healed or because God wants me healed? Am I praying for financial prosperity because it's what I want or because it's what God wants?* It will affect our whole approach to God if we settle that issue.

I remember once, some years back, a woman came to me and asked me to pray for her son who was hospitalized. He was about twelve years old and had a disease that was diagnosed as incurable. I was perfectly ready to pray with her, but without really thinking I said, "Have you surrendered your son to the Lord?"

When I asked her that simple question, she became hysterical. She thought I was trying to tell her that her son was going to die. I did not have that in mind. I simply wanted to point out to her that as long as she was pressing for her will, the will of God really could not come to pass. As long as she kept her hand over her son, God's hand could not touch him. As long as we are trying to force our own will through, we do not allow room for the will of God.

When you think about renouncing your own will and embracing the will of God, let me suggest you bear three truths in mind. First of all, God loves you more than you love yourself. Second, God understands you better than you understand yourself. And third, God wants only the best for you. When you truly yield to God's will, you will discover that it is what the Bible says it is: "good and acceptable and perfect" (Romans 12:2).

Reverent submission understands that prayer is not a way for us to get God to do what we want. When we say, "Your will be done," we are becoming instruments for God to do what He wants.

Consider what Paul said in Ephesians 3:20: "Now to Him who is able to do far more abundantly beyond all that we ask or think, according to the power that works within us . . ." (NASB). Another translation of that verse says: "Now to him who is able to do immeasurably more than all we ask or imagine, according to his power that is at work within us . . ." (NIV).

God's ability to answer our prayers goes abundantly, immeasurably beyond all that we ask or think. You might say, "How could that possibly be? What could be beyond anything that I could ask or think or imagine or reason?" The answer is: Whatever God wants to do.

You see, what God wants to do is far greater and far higher and far better than anything you or I could ever imagine or think of for ourselves. As long as we limit God to doing merely what we want, we miss what God wants. So in order to receive the best from God in our prayers, we have to come to God the way Jesus came—with reverent submission. We have to say, "God, not as I will, but as You will. God, I am not praying to be healed because I want to be healed, but because I believe You want me to be healed."

I lay sick in a hospital for one year and doctors were unable to heal me. I did not get out of the hospital healed until I had learned that God would heal me because He wanted me healed, not because I wanted to be healed. Can you bear that lesson in mind?

When you are praying with reverent submission to God's will, you are going to go far higher than you ever could by asserting your own will.

2. Have Faith

In the book of Hebrews we are told that there is one basic unvarying requirement for all who would approach God: "Without faith it is impossible to please God, because anyone who comes to him must believe that he exists and that he rewards those who earnestly seek him" (Hebrews 11:6, NIV).

Faith is an essential condition for approaching and being accepted by God. Anyone who comes to Him must believe. Furthermore, we are required to believe two things: that God exists and that He rewards those who earnestly seek Him.

Most people do not have trouble believing that God exists. If that were all, we would meet the condition of faith. But that is not all. We are also required to believe that He rewards those who earnestly seek Him.

Do you believe that? You may say, "Well, I try, but perhaps I am not seeking Him too well. I don't know much about doctrine or theology." I have good news for you. Faith of this kind is not primarily concerned with doctrine or theology. Rather it is about relationship. It involves trust in God as a

Person. It is confidence in His character, His reliability. In fact, get away from the thought of theology when you approach God in faith.

This is one of the reasons why this book starts with the importance of having a right picture of God—because that is what generates faith. We believe in God's goodness. We believe in His faithfulness. We believe in His reliability. This also helps us understand why the Bible teaches that unbelief is sinful. Unbelief casts aspersions on God's character. It paints a picture of God that is false and unattractive.

This requirement of faith is universal for any way of approaching God, but it is applied particularly to prayer. Look again, for instance, at Matthew 21:22: "All things you ask in prayer, believing, you will receive" (NASB). The key word is there in the middle: *believing.* Further, in 1 John 5:14 we read: "This is the confidence that we have in him, that, if we ask any thing according to his will, he heareth us" (KJV). If we have confidence in God Himself as a Person, confidence in His goodness, confidence in His character, then we can believe that He hears us.

How can we acquire the kind of faith that approaches God with confidence? Thank God that the New Testament does not merely tell us that we have to have faith; it also tells us how to get it. We find this in Romans 10:17: "Faith comes from hearing, and hearing by the word of Christ" (NASB).

This is a key verse for a life of prayer. It is, in fact, the verse that got me out of the hospital after that long year of illness. I really owe my health and my long life and my strength to the lessons about faith in this verse.

When I submitted myself to the Lord's will, I knew that His will was for me to be restored to health. I was lying there realizing that if I had faith God would heal me. But every time I came to that realization, my next thought was, *I don't have faith.*

Then one day the Holy Spirit directed me to Romans 10:17: "So faith comes from hearing." Suddenly I laid hold of two words: *Faith comes.* If you do not have it, you can get it!

How does faith come? Faith comes from hearing. It comes from listening to God. You see, prayer is not just talking *to* God; prayer is two-way communication *with* God. It is holding intimate personal conversation with Him. And actually, of the two, what God has to say is much more important than what we have to say.

God led me to Proverbs 4:20–22, what I came to refer to as "God's medicine bottle." I purposed to take God's Word as my medicine three times daily, after meals. After each main meal I would get away by myself, open my Bible, bow my head and say, "God, Your Word tells me that these words of Yours will be health to all my flesh. I take them now as my medicine in Jesus' name." In that unhealthy climate of the Sudan, God's Word brought me perfect permanent health.

Jesus told us that our Father already knows what we need (see Matthew 6:8). When we come to God telling Him we need things, we are not telling Him something that He does not already know. Prayer is getting into that attitude and relationship with God where you know you will receive what you need when you ask Him. That kind of faith comes from hearing what God has to say.

We read in the Bible that God appeared one night to David's son Solomon in a dream and said, "What do you want? I'll give it to you." Solomon gave a wise answer. He said, "Give Your servant a discerning heart." That is the English translation, but the Hebrew actually says a "hearing heart."

There is nothing more precious than a heart that hears God (see 1 Kings 3–4).

To help tune your heart to hear, I suggest that you pray with your Bible open. In fact, I suggest that you never begin a serious time of prayer without first reading your Bible. Why? First, because God speaks primarily through His Word. If you want to hear God, that is most often how you will hear Him. Second, because anything that does not agree with the Bible is not from God. Sometimes deceiving voices represent themselves as the voice of God, but they are not.

The first epistle of John explains this:

> This is the confidence which we have before Him, that, if we ask anything according to His will, He hears us. And if we know that He hears us in whatever we ask, we know that we have the requests which we have asked from Him.
>
> 1 John 5:14–15, NASB

The basis of successful praying is knowing that we are praying according to the will of God. The will of God is revealed primarily in the Bible. Thus, when we hear what God has to say, we grow in faith that our requests will be answered.

3. Pray in the Name of Jesus

Our next condition for answered prayer is very straightforward. The Bible tells us that we must pray in the name of Jesus. Let's look at just one example. Note also that these verses show how our relationship to God in the name of Jesus works both ways—in our asking and in God's giving. "Truly, truly, I say to you, if you ask the Father for anything in My name, He will give it to you. Until now you have asked for nothing in My name; ask and you will receive" (John 16:23–24, NASB).

What is implied when we pray in the name of Jesus? I suggest three truths.

First of all, when we pray in the name of Jesus we are coming to God on the basis of what Jesus has done on our behalf. First Peter 3:18 says: "For Christ also died for sins once for all, the just for the unjust, so that He might bring us to God" (NASB). Jesus paid the penalty for our sin when He died in our place. He also took our guilt and our condemnation, which opened the way for us to come to God without feeling guilty or ashamed. We now have the right of access to God.

In Ephesians 2:13, Paul says: "But now in Christ Jesus you who formerly were far off have been brought near by the blood of Christ" (NASB). The blood of Christ is the visible, eternal evidence of the sacrifice that Jesus made on our behalf. When we come in the name of Jesus, we come in the merits of the blood that He shed on our behalf.

We will discuss more thoroughly the blood of Jesus in chapter 7. Here let me just refer to Hebrews 12, which says this about the heavenlies: "You have come to . . . the city of the living God, the heavenly Jerusalem, . . . and to Jesus, the mediator of a new covenant, and to the sprinkled blood, which speaks better than the blood of Abel" (verses 22, 24, NASB).

This gives a beautiful comparison based on an incident in the Old Testament. You will recall from the story in Genesis that Cain murdered his brother, Abel. God spoke to Cain and said, "What have you done?" And when Cain pleaded ignorance and innocence, God said, "The voice of your brother's blood is crying to Me from the ground, crying for vengeance and justice" (see Genesis 4).

Here the writer of Hebrews says that the blood of Jesus is sprinkled on our behalf in the heavenlies, and it speaks better things than Abel's blood. In other words, the blood of Jesus is speaking of reconciliation, mercy, forgiveness, atonement.

When I find it hard to pray, one of my greatest consolations is that even if I do not know what to say, the blood of Jesus is always speaking in heaven on my behalf. That is part of what it means when I pray in the name of Jesus and recognize that I am coming to God on the basis of what Jesus has done for me.

The second truth that is implied when we pray in the name of Jesus is that we come on the basis of who Jesus Himself is, not who we are.

The writer of Hebrews says that we come before the Father with Jesus as our great High Priest:

> Therefore, brethren, since we have confidence to enter the holy place by the blood of Jesus, . . . and since we have a great priest over the house of God, let us draw near with a sincere heart in full assurance of faith.
>
> Hebrews 10:19, 21–22, NASB

In addition, John wrote: "My little children, I am writing these things to you so that you may not sin. And if anyone sins, we have an Advocate with the Father, Jesus Christ the righteous" (1 John 2:1, NASB). The word translated "advocate" means literally "someone called in alongside to help us and to plead our cause for us."

When we come in the name of Jesus, then we come with Him as our High Priest and our Advocate. As our High Priest, He offers up our prayers to God on our behalf—and because they are offered up by Jesus, we know that they reach God. As our Advocate, He speaks directly to God on our behalf.

He pleads our cause better than we could ever do ourselves. When we make mistakes and errors and even sin, we do not need to stay away from God and feel ashamed. We can come to God freely because of Jesus.

The third aspect to praying in the name of Jesus is this: It recognizes the relationship that we have with God through Jesus. Look at what Paul wrote:

> Blessed be the God and Father of our Lord Jesus Christ, who has blessed us with every spiritual blessing in the heavenly places in Christ, just as He chose us in Him before the foundation of the world, that we would be holy and blameless before Him. In love He predestined us to adoption as sons through Jesus Christ to Himself, according to the kind intention of His will, to the praise of the glory of His grace, which He freely bestowed on us in the Beloved.
>
> Ephesians 1:3–6, NASB

God had an eternal purpose in His heart and mind before time ever began or Creation ever took place. God foreknew us and determined that through Jesus Christ He would adopt us into His family as His children. All this was worked out in time and human history when Jesus came and died on our behalf.

The New King James Version translates that sixth verse this way: "To the praise of the glory of His grace, by which He made us accepted in the Beloved." I love that phrase *accepted in the Beloved.* That is what we are: We are accepted by God as His children when we come to Him in the Beloved, Jesus Christ. We are not accepted because of what we were but because of what Jesus is.

One of the biggest psychological and emotional problems of our contemporary culture is the problem of rejection.

So many people go through life feeling rejected, unwanted, second-rate—perhaps because of a wrong attitude of their parents or perhaps because of a wrong attitude of a husband or a wife in a marriage situation. Probably there is no greater wound than the wound of rejection. But the first step to healing that wound is to realize that when we come to God in Jesus, we are not rejected. God never rejects His children. We are accepted in the Beloved, and that makes all the difference in the way we come to God.

Once we come to God through Jesus on this basis, wonderful benefits are made available to us. First of all: "He who did not spare His own Son, but delivered Him over for us all, how will He not also with Him freely give us all things?" (Romans 8:32, NASB). Is that not a marvelous phrase? With Him, with Jesus, God will freely give us all things. But notice that it all depends on being *with Him*. When we are with Jesus we are entitled to everything as God's children. Without Him we have no claim upon Him at all.

Then this: "My God will supply all your needs according to His riches in glory in Christ Jesus" (Philippians 4:19, NASB). This means that no need of ours will go unsupplied; the supply comes from God's riches. I believe that God is rich enough to supply the needs of all His children, but the supply is in Christ Jesus.

4. Approach God Boldly

The next condition for approaching God in prayer in a way that will bring answers is to approach Him boldly. There are two ways to state this. Positively, it is with confidence. Negatively, it is without condemnation. Condemnation will always undermine confidence. Let's look at each of these.

With Confidence

Two Scriptures from the book of Hebrews tell us why we should approach God with confidence. Here is the first: "Therefore let us draw near with confidence to the throne of grace, so that we may receive mercy and find grace to help in time of need" (Hebrews 4:16, NASB).

We are praying to someone who is on a throne. A throne indicates a king. This is not merely *a* king, but *the* King. The King of all kings, the Lord of all lords, the Supreme Ruler of the universe, the One who said, "All authority has been given to *Me* in heaven and on earth" (Matthew 28:18, emphasis added). We are praying to someone who has both the authority and the power to do what we ask. Let's lift our eyes from ourselves and our own needs and problems and look up to that glorious throne.

Then it is a throne of grace. *Grace* is one of the key words in the New Testament. It always stands for something that goes beyond anything we can earn or achieve by our own efforts. Because it is a throne of grace, we are not limited to what we deserve or to what we can achieve or to what our own efforts can accomplish for us.

One awareness I have always had in my Christian life is that I stand in need of the mercy of God. This Scripture encourages me to believe that if I ever come for mercy, mercy is what I will receive. I believe the reason some people do not receive mercy is simply that they never see their need of it and come in faith to receive it.

And then we are to come for help in time of need. We are not to look at the circumstances. We are not to say, "Well, the situation is so grave and the problems are so great that there is nothing to be done about it." It is just at a time of need, it is just when the problems are great, that God invites us to come.

Look again at this beautiful Scripture from Hebrews that encourages us to come with confidence: "Therefore, brethren, since we have confidence to enter the holy place by the blood of Jesus, . . . let us draw near with a sincere heart in full assurance of faith" (Hebrews 10:19, 22, NASB).

Confidence. Full assurance. Everything suggests boldness—boldness based upon the fact that the blood of Jesus has been shed and has been sprinkled in the very presence of God. The blood is now speaking on our behalf even when we do not know how to pray.

You will notice that both of those phrases from Hebrews say, "Let us." That indicates two aspects. First of all, it indicates a decision. Second, it is a plural decision; it is made by more than one person. Sometimes we need to come to Him collectively, corporately—not just as an individual, but as a member of a body that is praying together with us.

Without Condemnation

The positive side of coming to God boldly is to come with confidence. The other side is that we come without condemnation. Several passages of Scripture speak about the need to be free from condemnation.

Here is one from the Psalms: "If I regard wickedness in my heart, the Lord will not hear" (Psalm 66:18, NASB). To "regard iniquity in my heart" means that I am conscious of something that condemns me. Every time I try to approach God with faith, Satan reminds me of this flaw that is not right, that has not been dealt with. It might be a sin that has not been confessed, or, if it has been confessed, I have not claimed and received God's forgiveness. If I am conscious of this flaw in my heart, I will not receive that which I pray for. I must remove the consciousness of sin

39

from within my heart and come boldly before His throne (see Hebrews 4:16).

Basically this is done by faith, because if we confess our sin, God "is faithful and just to forgive us our sins and to cleanse us from all unrighteousness" (1 John 1:9). Once we confess, repent and trust God for the forgiveness and the cleansing that He has promised, we must not go on worrying about our sins. If we do, if we remain "sin conscious" as we pray, God will not hear our prayers. If I regard iniquity in my heart, the Lord will not hear me. But do you know what the psalmist goes on to say? "The Lord has heard me." In other words, he rose above Satan's attempt to condemn him.

John expressed the same thought: "Beloved, if our heart does not condemn us, we have confidence before God; and whatever we ask we receive from Him" (1 John 3:21–22, NASB). We have to get rid of any attitude that suggests some kind of righteousness in ourselves. We have no righteousness of our own. We must come to a place where we are trusting in God's faithfulness, and that produces confidence.

Again, in Romans 8:1, Paul said: "Therefore there is now no condemnation for those who are in Christ Jesus" (NASB). In the remainder of the chapter he painted the most glorious picture of all the blessings and privileges and benefits of the life that is filled and controlled by the Holy Spirit. We gain entry into that chapter and that kind of life as we lay aside condemnation.

I think the trouble with most Christians is that they do not know whether they are righteous or not. That is the truth. If I have been justified by faith in Jesus Christ, I have been made righteous with His righteousness. And if I know that, stand on it and live according to it, no judgment due to the wicked shall ever touch me.

Now, that does not mean that the Christian will not have trouble in this world: We will be persecuted for righteousness' sake. The Bible says that the godly in Christ Jesus shall suffer persecution. But there is a vital basic difference between persecution for righteousness' sake and judgment for wickedness. Persecution for righteousness comes upon the righteous from the wicked. Judgment for wickedness comes from God, who is righteous, upon the wicked.

We are all called to endure persecution. None of us who are believers, however, should ever endure God's judgment upon the wicked. If you really understand that, you will likely heave a sigh of relief. But as I say, the majority of Christians really do not know where they stand.

In Luke 21:36 Jesus spoke about the close of this age. Right at the end of His message, speaking to His disciples, He said, "Watch therefore, and pray always that you may be counted worthy to escape all these things that will come to pass, and to stand before the Son of Man." He indicated that it was the will of God for His disciples to escape the judgments of God that were coming upon the wicked earth. That is in line with the whole teaching of Scripture. But He was telling them, "You had better be watching and praying. Otherwise you will not qualify to escape."

And He also said, "Watch . . . and pray . . . that you may be counted worthy." Were you worthy to be saved? No, you were saved by grace. You did not merit it; you could not deserve it. But when you have been saved, you are required to lead such a life of righteousness that it would be unrighteous of God to judge you with the wicked. That is the Christian life.

At the end of this age, be careful not to let the lines get blurred because you might be on the wrong side. As we will see in chapter 9, when we learn about God's purpose in prayer for the Church, there is a wider and wider gulf growing between the righteous and the unrighteous, the filthy and the holy. The unrighteous and the filthy are going to get worse. The righteous and the holy are going to get better (see Revelation 22:11). You had better know which company you are in.

There must come a time when we lay aside every attempt to justify ourselves and say, "I receive by faith the righteousness of Jesus Christ imputed to me by my faith in Him according to the Word of God. I will not worry about my merits. I will not worry about my sins. I will not parade my good deeds. I will not blush for my bad deeds. I will not examine and analyze my own heart all the time to see if I am good enough. I will trust God that the blood of Jesus has cleansed me from all sin. And now I am going boldly right to the throne, right into the holiest place of all."

That is a glorious way of access.

The book of Esther gives a beautiful picture of coming into the presence of a king. This was a time of tremendous national and personal crisis: The lives of her people were at stake, and the king had not invited her to come. She took her life in her hands by deciding to appeal to him. After fasting for three days, she put on her royal attire and went into the king's presence. He received her and gave her her request. Notice, she went in like a queen, not like a beggar. That is how Christ wants His Church to come to Him—like a queen, believing that she will be received because of His grace and His righteousness.

5. Have the Right Motive

The next condition for answered prayer is to pray with the right motive.

Religious people, like the Pharisees, tend to focus on externals. They are concerned about the way people dress, the entertainment they enjoy, the things they eat. It is hard for religious people, who work from the outside in, to realize that God starts with what is inside and works outward.

When God sent Samuel to the house of Jesse to anoint one of his sons as the future king of Israel, Jesse brought forward seven sons, all of whom were fine, handsome, strong, upstanding young men. Each time Samuel saw one of these sons he thought, *This must be the one.* But each time the Lord corrected him and said, *That's not the one.* Then the Lord gave him this explanation: "God sees not as man sees, for man looks at the outward appearance, but the LORD looks at the heart" (1 Samuel 16:7, NASB).

God searches the thoughts and intents of our hearts, and discerns our motives. He is not concerned merely with what we ask for when we pray; He is also concerned as to why we want it. This is explained more fully in this verse: "You do not have because you do not ask. You ask and do not receive, because you ask with wrong motives, so that you may spend it on your pleasures" (James 4:2–3, NASB).

One simple reason why we do not have things God wants us to have is because we do not ask. But if we do ask and still do not receive, it could be because we are praying with wrong motives. Particularly, the motive that James said is wrong is that we may spend it on our pleasures. In other words, if our prayers are self-centered, our motives are wrong. We are simply aiming to get something for our own creature comfort and personal satisfaction.

So we ask, What is the right motive for praying? Jesus stated it clearly: "Whatever you ask in My name, that will I do, so that the Father may be glorified in the Son" (John 14:13, NASB).

Jesus gave a comprehensive promise: Whatever we ask in His name, He will do. But the basis on which He will do it is this: "that the Father may be glorified in the Son." The right motive for praying is that the answer may bring glory to God. This is actually the right motive for all we do. The life of righteousness that is based on faith gives glory to God.

We can look at this from the opposite side. What is the essence of sin? It is not necessarily robbing a bank or committing adultery or doing something terrible in the eyes of religious people. The essence of sin is choosing not to live for God's glory, denying Him the glory that is rightfully due to Him.

Paul described in his letter to the Romans how the whole human race has turned away from God and descended into a life of ignorance and wickedness—in his word, futility. He noted the steps that led to this awful descent into the abyss of darkness: "Although they knew God, they neither glorified him as God nor gave thanks to him, but their thinking became futile and their foolish hearts were darkened" (Romans 1:21, NIV).

What are the first two steps down? The first is the failure to glorify God. The second is the failure to be thankful. Anyone who takes those two first steps downward is set on a slippery path that leads to a condition that ultimately is too horrible to think about. We have to be careful in praying that we do not make those errors.

God wants each of us set free from the negative pull of sin and restored to the right motive and the right purpose of living. When we come to Him and pray with that motive—that God may be glorified in answering prayer that is offered in the name of His Son, Jesus Christ—then He says something truly wonderful. He says that all of His promises are made available to us: "For no matter how many promises God has made, they are 'Yes' in Christ. And so through him the

'Amen' is spoken by us to the glory of God" (2 Corinthians 1:20, NIV).

Is that not staggering? Every promise that fits my situation and meets my needs is for me, now, if I claim it in the name of Jesus and if I claim it to the glory of God. No matter how many promises God has made—and I have heard it estimated that there are eight thousand promises of God in Scripture—they are all "Yes" in Christ.

The response of faith is that to God's "Yes," we say, "Amen, to the glory of God." It is our "Amen" that clinches God's "Yes" and makes the promise ours.

6. Forgive Those Who Have Hurt You

In the Sermon on the Mount, one of the things Jesus taught us to say, as I suppose we all know, is this: "Forgive us our debts [our trespasses], as we forgive our debtors [those who trespass against us]" (Matthew 6:12). Forgive us as we forgive others. What we might not realize is that this is an important condition for receiving answers to prayer.

I have found in counseling, and dealing with people in general, that this is one of the most common sources of blockage and frustration in the spiritual life and of failure to receive answers to prayer. Usually it involves one specific person. I was talking once with someone who sought help, and I said, "Is there anybody you haven't forgiven?"

She said, "Yes," and mentioned a distinguished person in the judiciary department of the United States. I said, "If you want release, you'll have to forgive him. There's no alternative. If you don't forgive him, God doesn't forgive you." Forgive us as we forgive others.

Jesus has limited us to asking God for forgiveness only in the proportion that we forgive others. Are you willing to forgive?

Remember this, my friend, forgiveness is not an emotion; it is a decision. I call it "tearing up the IOU." Somebody owes you three thousand dollars. All right. Tear up the IOU. Because do you know how much you owe God? Six million dollars. Do you want Him to tear up that IOU? You tear up yours; He will tear up His. That is His unvarying law. You cannot change God. He demands that we forgive if we want Him to forgive us.

The last petition in the Lord's Prayer is a petition for deliverance from Satan. "Deliver us from the evil one" (Matthew 6:13) is the correct translation. You and I have no right to pray for deliverance till we have forgiven others as we would have God forgive us.

Jesus also said, "And whenever you stand praying, if you have anything against anyone, forgive him" (Mark 11:25). Now that does not leave out anything or anybody. When you pray, forgive, "that your Father in heaven may also forgive you your trespasses. But if you do not forgive, neither will your Father in heaven forgive your trespasses" (verses 25–26). This is absolutely clear—and it is spoken to Christians, those who have God as their heavenly Father. Before you and I pray, we must forgive. It will do no good to try to approach God in prayer with unforgiveness in our hearts against anybody about anything.

7. Be Directed by the Holy Spirit

The last two conditions—be directed by the Holy Spirit and ask according to God's Word—help us understand how to pray the will of God. We will see that the power of the Holy Spirit works through our prayers only insofar as they are in line with the Word of God.

Let's begin with this verse: "For as many as are led by the Spirit of God, these are sons of God" (Romans 8:14). That is a continuing present tense in the Greek. As many as are *regularly led* by the Spirit of God, they are the sons of God. How do you live daily as a son or daughter of God in this world? It is by being regularly, continually led by the Holy Spirit.

Later on in Romans 8 the apostle Paul applied this truth about the leading of the Holy Spirit in the Christian life specifically to prayer:

> Likewise the Spirit also helps in our weaknesses [infirmities]. For we do not know what we should pray for as we ought, but the Spirit Himself makes intercession for us with groanings which cannot be uttered. Now He who searches the hearts knows what the mind of the Spirit is, because He [the Spirit] makes intercession for the saints according to the will of God.
>
> Verses 26–27

Paul said that the Spirit comes to the help of our weaknesses or infirmities, and that we all have a certain specific infirmity. It is not a physical sickness; it is not a disease. It is part of our carnal nature. What is this weakness? We do not know what to pray for as we ought. Or to state it another way, we do not always know what to pray for, and even if we do, many times we still do not know how to pray for it. You might know that your son needs prayer or your friend needs prayer, but you still do not know how to pray.

What is God's solution? The Spirit of God comes to your help in this infirmity. How? He takes over and makes intercession through you, praying according to the will of God. So when we do not know how to pray according to the mind of God, when we are faced with a need that we do not know how to pray about, what do we do? We turn to the Holy Spirit and say, "Holy Spirit, You take over and pray through me."

This is one of the glorious blessings of being truly baptized with the Holy Spirit. It is why I believe the baptism with the Holy Spirit must be consummated by supernatural utterance where the Holy Spirit speaks and not the believer. Or rather the Holy Spirit gives the believer a language to speak that the believer does not know. When the believer has yielded himself in this manner, the Spirit Himself prays through him, making intercession for him with groanings that cannot be uttered. He prays for the saints according to the will of God. He prays the prayer that God wants to hear and wants to answer.

How wonderful to realize that when we do not know how to pray, we can turn to God and let His Spirit loose! When He prays through us in unknown tongues we are praying the right prayer. We know that it is the right prayer because the Holy Spirit is giving us that prayer, and He prays according to the revealed will of God. He takes over our vocal organs and our inner nature, and He holds a prayer meeting inside us! This is God's glorious provision for every believer in Christ.

I remember once when my first wife, Lydia, and I were in Denmark, which was her native land, at the end of October. We were planning a trip to Britain for the month of November. One morning as we were praying together sitting up in bed as we often did, she launched out in prayer and I heard her say this: "Lord, give us fine weather all the time we're in Britain."

Well, I nearly fell out of the bed. I said to her afterward, "Do you know what you prayed?" She shook her head. I said, "You prayed for God to give us fine weather all the time we're in Britain." She did not even recall praying it. It did not come from her mind at all—it was given by the Spirit.

I said, "You know what Britain is like in November. It's cold, damp, misty, foggy—utterly unpleasant." We had lived in Britain long enough to know what November is like.

But do you know what happened? We went to Britain and the whole month of November was like spring. I have never seen a November like that in all the years I have lived there. When we left, the last day of November, we said to our friends who had come to see us off at the airport, "You'd better look out now—the weather's going to change!"

When we have come to the end of our limited understanding, when we have used up our own poor mental resources, what do we do? We turn it over to the Holy Spirit. He is equal to the task. My first wife's favorite text on prayer was, "Open thy mouth wide, and I will fill it" (Psalm 81:10, KJV). Just give the Holy Spirit your mouth and let Him fill it. He is longing to pray through you.

The Bible says we should pray always, pray without ceasing (see 1 Thessalonians 5:17; Ephesians 6:18). Can any of us in our own natural strength and understanding pray always and without ceasing? Absolutely not. But when we let the Holy Spirit in and turn it over to Him, He conducts a prayer meeting 24 hours a day.

You can pray in your sleep, you know. This is a fact. Many people have been heard to speak in tongues hours on end while lying in sleep. In the Song of Solomon the bride says, "I sleep, but my heart is awake" (Song of Solomon 5:2). That is one of the beauties of the Bride of Christ: Her heart stays awake praying in the Spirit while her mind and her body are getting refreshing sleep. You can spend hours in prayer and wake up fresh as a daisy in the morning. This is praying on the level of God's revealed will. It is letting the Holy Spirit help our infirmities; He can take over and pray the way God wants us to pray.

As we noted earlier, Paul said that God is able to do exceeding abundantly above all that we could ever figure or reason or think of asking with our natural minds. When I have thought of the highest I can think of, when I reach the limit of my natural thinking and reasoning as to what God can and should do, then I can let the Holy Spirit in and move on to a higher plane in prayer. And it is that level of prayer on which every child of God has the right to live and move and have his being.

8. Ask According to God's Word

The last of the basic conditions for answered prayer is praying in accordance with the Word of God. This is intimately related to the previous condition—being directed by the Holy Spirit. You see, the great issue in prayer is the will of God. If I am praying according to the will of God, then, as we have seen in Scripture, I know that God hears me. And if I know that God hears me, I know that I have the petition that I ask.

How do I know the will of God? Where is the will of God revealed? The answer is in His Word. The great revelation of the will of God is the Word of God. And the Word of God is packed from beginning to end with divine promises. The apostle Peter calls them "exceedingly great and precious promises" (2 Peter 1:4). And do you know what those promises are? *The promises of God are the will of God.*

Thus, when you find a promise that relates to your situation and meets your need, that promise is God's will for you. God never promised anything that was not His will; anything else would be inconsistent. Suppose you came to Him and said, "Lord, You promised." He would not say, "Yes, I promised but I don't want to do it."

This last condition, then, is the great secret that clinches our life of prayer: We pray according to God's will as revealed in His Word.

Let's look at two examples that illustrate this. The first is in the Old Testament; the second is in the New Testament. In 1 Chronicles we find an incident in the life of David. At this juncture David was established in his kingdom. He was victorious in battle, he had peace, he had abundance, he had a beautiful house to live in. As he sat in his beautiful house and thought about things, this idea came to him: *Here am I living in this beautiful house of cedar, but the Ark of God is still in a tent* (see 1 Chronicles 17:1).

So he said to the prophet Nathan, "I'm going to build a house for the Ark of the Lord."

Nathan said, "That's a wonderful idea. Go ahead and do it." But that night God spoke to Nathan and said, "Go and tell my servant David: You are not to build a house for Me; your son is going to do that. But do you know what I'm going to do for you? I am going to build *you* a house."

Is that not wonderful? That is also an example of "exceeding abundantly above." David tried to think of the greatest thing he could do for God, and God responded with something greater. You understand that the word *house* in the Bible does not mean primarily a building, but a family, a household. God was promising David that his posterity and his line would endure, and also that one of his sons would sit upon his throne and rule over all Israel and over all nations forever and ever.

When he got the message, "King David went in and sat before the LORD" (1 Chronicles 17:16).

I like that picture of sitting before the Lord. I do not know how it is with you, but if I kneel too long I get distinctly uncomfortable. There is nothing in the Bible that tells us we can only pray kneeling. In fact, on the Day of Pentecost when the Holy Spirit fell they were sitting.

So David came and relaxed before Almighty God and said something on this order: "God, You have been so good to me, I want to take a little time to appreciate You and thank You for Your goodness." Then David said this: "And now, O LORD, the word which You have spoken concerning Your servant and concerning his house, let it be established forever, and *do as You have said*" (17:23, emphasis added).

Those five short words of one syllable each contain the essence of effective praying. *Do as You have said*. Lord, You said it; please do it. If God has said He will do it and you ask Him to do it, you can know He is going to do it. His promises are the revelation of His will.

Do you see the beauty of this prayer? Let the thing that You have spoken, Lord, be established. I did not speak it, Lord; I did not think of it. It is far above what I can think of, wish for or ask. But, Lord, You said it; please do it.

Notice also that David had the right motive in praying. In verse 24 we read: "Let it be established, that Your name may be magnified forever." David did not ask that he would be glorified, but that the name of the Lord would be glorified. This is a perfect pattern prayer. "Let the thing that You have spoken be established. Do as You have said, that Your name may be magnified forever."

This is the great key to answered prayer. If we do not know what God has promised in His Word, how can we go to Him and say, "Lord, You promised; please do it"? We must bring the Word and the Spirit together in our prayers, because then the whole creative power and ability of Almighty God is available to us.

Think about it: this is how God brought the universe into being. "By the word of the LORD the heavens were made, and all the host of them by the breath [or Spirit] of His mouth" (Psalm 33:6). The Word and the Spirit of God together brought all creation into being. When you and I bring the Spirit and the Word together, then He will do exceeding abundantly above all that we can ask or think.

Here is a New Testament example. I sometimes ask people, "Apart from the personal events in the life of the Lord Jesus, what would you consider to be the greatest single miracle that ever took place in the life of a human being?" I have received a variety of answers. Sometimes people say, for instance, the experience of Lazarus being raised after four days in the tomb.

I would not argue with any of the answers, but my personal feeling is that the greatest single miracle that ever took place in the life of an ordinary human being was when the Virgin Mary conceived in her womb and became the mother of the Son of God.

And how did it come about? When she said one simple phrase.

The angel told Mary what was ordained of God. He then explained that the power of the Holy Spirit would overshadow her and said, "For with God nothing will be impossible" (Luke 1:37). In the margin of my Bible is an alternative translation: "No word of God shall be without power." Or it could be rendered: Every word of God contains within it the power for its own fulfillment.

Mary received the word of God brought from the angel. And as she received it, she received the power that brought fulfillment. Here is her response, and our pattern for prayer in the beautiful King James Version: "Behold the handmaid of the Lord; be it unto me according to thy word" (Luke 1:38, KJV). With those words the greatest miracle in human experience was ushered in.

You and I can pray on this level as well. If we want the great things, the "exceeding abundantly above all that you can ask or think" things, the answer is to pray according to God's Word.

These two prayers of David and of Mary are intimately connected with the coming of the Lord Jesus. David was the Lord's great ancestor, the one God promised would always have a son on the throne. The promise was fulfilled through the birth of Jesus, conceived in the womb of the Virgin Mary. In each case the key to answered prayer was the same. "God, You said it; You do it."

You will never pray a higher or more effective prayer than when, guided by the Holy Spirit, you go to the Word, find the promise that relates to you and your situation and say, "Lord, You said it; You do it." If you do this, having met the previous conditions for prayer, you will discover the secret of effective praying.

3

KINGDOM PRAYING ON EARTH

If my people, who are called by my name, will humble themselves and pray . . . then will I hear from heaven.

2 Chronicles 7:14, NIV

Thus far we have laid a foundation of three important
and related truths. First, we learned that God has made
us a Kingdom of priests. As such, our responsibility
is to rule by prayer. The Bible reveals that this world is not
really ruled by presidents and governors and dictators. They
only seem to rule. The people who really rule the world are
those who know how to pray.

Second, we learned that, to be effective, we must meet
certain conditions for approaching God in prayer in a way
that will bring answers.

Third, we learned as part of those conditions that the
Spirit of God and the Word of God always work together.
The power of the Holy Spirit works through our prayers only

insofar as they are in line with the Word of God. This means that to pray effectively we must know what the Bible says.

Now let's take what we have learned so far and apply it to a specific example—an important example. This is what Paul wrote to Timothy:

> Therefore I exhort first of all that supplications, prayers, intercessions, and giving of thanks be made for all men, for kings and all who are in authority, that we may lead a quiet and peaceable life in all godliness and reverence. For this is good and acceptable in the sight of God our Savior, who desires all men to be saved and to come to the knowledge of the truth.
>
> 1 Timothy 2:1–4

This is one of the most logical passages that I know of in the Bible. It unfolds a series of thoughts and gives us sound and logical reasons for what it is saying.

Paul wrote this letter to Timothy to instruct him in the order and discipline of a local congregation. He said that the first great activity of a local group is supplications, prayers, intercessions and giving of thanks. If we were to use one collective noun for those different phrases, it would be *prayer*. So the primary activity of believers meeting together in fellowship as they begin to minister to the Lord is prayer. Prayer is basic.

This agrees with Isaiah 56:7 where God said this to believers who had gathered in assembly: "My house shall be called a house of prayer for all nations." In other words, not only are we to pray, but our prayers are to be as wide in their outreach as the love and the mercy of God; the offer of the Gospel is for all.

Then Paul revealed the first theme of prayer. At the end of the opening verse he said, generally, prayer should be given on behalf of all men, but then he explained for whom we are to pray first. Out of the whole human race, for whom are we to pray first? Is it for the missionary? The evangelist? The sick? No, and this is where the great majority of Christians are out of line with the revealed will of God. They do not put God's priority first.

God says when we come together in a local congregation in prayer, or when two or three are met together, the first thing that He wants us to pray for is kings and all who are in authority. I would say, using modern phraseology, that this relates today to government. Have you realized that your primary responsibility in prayer is to pray for the government of your nation? My observation is that in multitudes of churches the people never think about that, even once a month. Yet Paul put it first.

What are we to ask God to do for and through the government? "That we may lead a quiet and peaceable life in all godliness and reverence." Let's ask ourselves this simple question. Does the government we live under affect the life we lead? Obviously it affects it in many ways continually. So if we want to lead a good life, logic and self-interest alone would indicate that we should pray for our government.

What are we to ask that the government will achieve? That it will achieve a situation in which we who are under the government may lead a quiet and peaceable life in all godliness and reverence. In other words, we are to pray that the government will do its job properly. Or more simply still, we are to pray for good government.

How many of us can say that we are leading a quiet and peaceable life in all godliness and reverence? Some years ago in San Francisco I sat next to two diplomatic officials from Hong Kong at breakfast. I asked them in a conversational way what it is like in Hong Kong, expecting them to tell me about the Communist threat and so on. What impressed them, however, was that in Hong Kong a woman can walk alone at any hour of the night. That was not the case in San Francisco—even in the daytime in some areas.

We know this is true. In most major American cities today a woman cannot walk alone with safety and unconcern. And in many areas neither can a man. Are we leading a quiet and peaceable life in all godliness and reverence?

In order to become an American citizen I learned that the center of all American institutions is the Constitution. As I read through the Constitution and its amendments in the form in which it is provided for those intending to become citizens, I came up with this conclusion. The basic purpose of the American Constitution, as devised by its founders, was to create a situation in the United States of America where we can lead a quiet and peaceable life in all godliness and reverence.

I really believe that those words sum up as accurately as is possible the basic intent of the American Constitution. If that intent is achieved, I believe we can say that we have good government. In other words, the function of good government by American standards is to provide a framework, a situation of law and order and administration, in which each one of us can go about our daily life and business leading a quiet and peaceable life in all godliness and reverence. I really am convinced that the founding fathers would have accepted that as their primary objective in framing the Constitution.

In the next verse of our Scripture, we read: "This is good and acceptable in the sight of God our Savior." *This*— meaning good government—is tremendously important. It is God's will.

Then Paul told us one basic reason why God approves of good government, why it is His will. He wrote: "[God] desires all men to be saved and to come to the knowledge of the truth" (verse 4). I pointed out already that God's mercy and love are outstretched to the whole human race. God wants all people to be saved, but they cannot be saved without coming to the knowledge of the truth. And they cannot come to the knowledge of the truth unless the truth—the truth of the Gospel—is presented to them.

So for that very simple and logical reason, God wants the truth of the Gospel proclaimed to everyone everywhere. All we have to do then is ask ourselves one more question. Which one makes it easier to proclaim the Gospel: good government or bad government? I think the answer is too obvious to need a lot of explanation. Bad government hinders the preaching of the Gospel. Good government, in many different ways, facilitates the preaching of the Gospel. So good government is the revealed will of God.

Here, then, is our basis for successful prayer in this particular example. As a Kingdom of priests, we know that it is our responsibility to rule the world for God by our prayers. We strive earnestly to meet the conditions for approaching God in prayer—we come to Him in reverent submission, in faith and in line with the other requirements. We then study the Word as guided by the Holy Spirit, and discern that good government is God's will. If, therefore, we pray for good government, we know that God hears us. And if we know that God hears us, we have what we asked for.

Now let's turn that around. If we do not have good government, and I am only saying *if*—each one of us has to decide if our governments are effective or efficient or whatever standard we use—but *if* we do not have good government, what is the reason? There are only two possible reasons if we believe what the Bible teaches.

The first reason is that we have not prayed as we ought to. I suppose that in the United States that applies to well over half the professing Christians. They never really pray intelligently and with real concern for the government. They shrug their shoulders and offer a lot of criticism. Let me take a moment to point out that there is no authority in Scripture to criticize the government, but there is an obligation to pray for it.

The second possible reason is that we have prayed but without knowing the will of God. It is only when we pray knowing God's will that we can say we have what we pray for. In this instance, we know that good government is the will of God because it facilitates the preaching of the Gospel, which is the primary purpose of God for our world.

Why do we Christians find it so hard to believe that so much depends on our praying? We take the attitude that what goes on is beyond our control; there is nothing we can do about the government—or prejudice or hatred or whatever ills we see around us. We shrug our shoulders. We criticize. We complain. But we fail to pray. This is why we see worldwide moral and ethical decline, both in leadership and in national culture. We have not understood the limitless possibilities of praying according to God's will as revealed in His Word. Because of this, we fail to rule in God's Kingdom the way He intends.

Three Metaphors for Prayer

Suppose we acknowledge that we Christians have failed to exercise our potential influence for good in all aspects of our lives. Is there anything that we can do to remedy this situation?

My reply is yes. The Bible has a clear and practical answer to this question, but before we turn to it, let us first face up to the full extent of our responsibility as Christians to exercise a unique and decisive influence on—that is, to rule—the society in which we live.

Jesus gave guidelines for us in the Sermon on the Mount. He used three metaphors in succession: salt, light, a city on a hill. Here is what He said:

> You are the salt of the earth; but if the salt has become tasteless, how can it be made salty again? It is no longer good for anything, except to be thrown out and trampled under foot by men. You are the light of the world. A city set on a hill cannot be hidden.
>
> Matthew 5:13–14, NASB

Let's look at the particular significance of each metaphor. I would like to take them in the reverse order to which Jesus mentioned them.

First of all, we Christians are a city set on a hill. What does that mean? I think the word that sums it up best is *conspicuous*. We can be seen from all angles at all times. We are always being watched. The moment you let people know that you believe in Jesus Christ, that you are a committed follower of His, that you attend such and such a church, people begin to look at you in a special way. They analyze your life, your conduct, your behavior.

They are thinking: *Is it real or is it just a religious act that he's putting on?* They do not look at you in church, but they will look at you in places like the office or the factory or the kitchen. Jesus was saying that all of us who profess faith in Him are collectively just as visible as a city on a hill.

Secondly, Jesus said that we are the light of the world. There is one important thing about light: It has no substitute. Nothing else can take its place. That is true of us as followers of Christ—there is no substitute for us; no one else can take our places or do our jobs. Also, light is the only answer to darkness. That is to say, where light comes, there is not much of a problem with darkness.

The third picture that Jesus used is that of the salt of the earth. Now salt is familiar, of course, and much could be said about it. I will just point out two main functions of salt: to give flavor and to hold back corruption.

If food is not very tasty or somewhat bland—maybe you are eating an egg—what do you do? You sprinkle salt on it. The salt gives flavor to that which otherwise might be flavorless.

If we are the salt of the earth, we are like little granules sprinkled across the earth's surface. Our responsibility is to give the earth flavor. Flavor for whom? For God. Our presence should make the earth acceptable to God in a way that it would not be acceptable to Him if we were not here as Christians living out our lives in His grace and love, worshiping and praising Him and praying according to His will. Our presence makes all the difference as to how He views the earth. I believe the earth will discover this one day when God takes us all out in the great event known as the Rapture, but that day has not come yet. We are responsible in the meantime to be salt.

The second function of salt is to hold back corruption. In the days before refrigeration, people preserved meat by salting it. Likewise it is our responsibility to hold back the forces of corruption—moral corruption, social corruption, political corruption—until God's purposes of mercy and grace have been worked out for this world of ours.

Now suppose we fail in our function as salt—to give flavor and to hold back corruption. Listen to what Jesus said: "If the salt does not do its job, it is good for nothing anymore."

Do you realize that applies to us? If we are not doing what we should, we are good for nothing anymore! We might expect "to be thrown out and trampled under foot." How would you feel if that happened?

You see, it is a sobering fact that millions and millions of people across the earth's surface today would count it their greatest privilege to trample Christians underfoot—particularly, perhaps, the Christians of America. God is not going to come down and trample us underfoot Himself, but He will turn us over to those who hate Christianity and all that it stands for. And the most bitter reflection of such a moment will be, "We deserved it. Jesus warned us. We didn't listen. He said that if we didn't serve as salt, we would be thrown out and trampled underfoot."

The Remedy

As I mentioned, I believe that there is a remedy for our general failure to exercise our potential for good. I believe that God in His mercy offers us a way to change the situation for the better. The key verse that gives us direction is a familiar one: "If my people, who are called by my name, will humble themselves and pray and seek my face and turn from their wicked ways, then will I hear from heaven and will forgive their sin and will heal their land" (2 Chronicles 7:14, NIV).

Let's consider for a moment of whom that is spoken. God says, "My people, who are called by my name." The Hebrew actually says *upon whom my name is called*. That describes you and me as Christians exactly. We are Christians because the name of the Lord Jesus Christ is called upon us. We are His people. That being the case, God requires four things of us. If we do those four things, He will do three things.

Let's start with the three things that God says He will do. Here are the first two: "I will hear from heaven and will forgive their sin." God is not committing to hear all prayers, but He says that if we meet His conditions then He will hear our prayers and forgive our sin. Be sure to notice that He is talking about the sin of His people. We need to understand that. Our sins are standing between us and God's intervention.

The third thing that God says He will do is "heal their land." Does the land in most parts of the world need healing? Speaking as an American, I would say that the American nation has never needed healing more desperately at any time in its history than it does now. God's promise to heal our land is surely a promise for us today. But remember: It is a conditional promise.

What four things, then, does God require us to do? First comes humility. Scripture says, "God resists the proud, but gives grace to the humble" (1 Peter 5:5). We can begin to pray, but if we pray out of pride and arrogance and self-righteousness, God does not hear our prayers. When we have humbled ourselves, then we can follow His second requirement and pray.

The third point is to seek God's face. I think this means more than, say, a prayer meeting that begins at 7:30 and concludes at 9:00. Seeking God's face means we pray until we know we have met Him and the answer is on the way.

And fourth, we have to turn from our wicked ways. Let's face the fact that *our* wicked ways have caused the problems in our lands. Our prayerlessness, our lack of witnessing, our lack of forthright open righteousness that challenges the ungodly and the unbeliever—God puts the responsibility for change upon us.

Now that we understand some biblical principles to follow for getting answers to prayer, let's look at different specific ways to pray—ways like petition and intercession. I like to think of various types of prayer as part of a great symphony. That is the topic of our next chapter—twelve different types of prayer, harmonious ways, if you will, of putting these principles to work.

4

TWELVE DIFFERENT TYPES
OF PRAYER

Again I say to you that if two of you agree on earth concerning anything that they ask, it will be done for them by My Father in heaven. For where two or three are gathered together in My name, I am there in the midst of them.

Matthew 18:19–20

This Scripture gives us an important principle for putting to use our foundations for effective prayer. It is what I call "the prayer symphony," and I use the word *symphony* deliberately. The word *agree* used here is actually a musical term. It is taken from the Greek word *sumphoneo*, and gives us the English word *symphony* by direct derivation. The basic concept is one of harmony.

The English words *gathered together* mean, literally, "have been led together." When we talk about being led in prayer, we come to the question, Led by whom? The answer is given in Romans 8:14: "For as many as are led by the Spirit of God, these are sons of God." Just as the Holy Spirit leads us to understand God's will in Scripture, so He leads us in praying it back to God.

Jesus was saying in this verse, then, that any time two or three have been led together by the Holy Spirit into a meeting place, which is the name of Jesus, then they can count on His presence. Additionally, if these ones shall symphonize—come together in perfect harmony—concerning anything that they shall ask, then it will be done for them.

Notice that Jesus did not say, "When two Baptists meet together, I'll be there" or "When three Pentecostals or Catholics or Methodists meet together, I'll be there." A lot of people misapply this Scripture. They talk about the presence of Jesus when, believe me, He is a long way off. He has tied Himself only to those who are led by the Spirit of God to come into His name.

God also gives us here, I think, a new vision of corporate prayer. It might be the case that two or three of us are sitting together in a group—our traditional view of this verse. But it might also be the case that we are scattered physically in different places in solitary prayer closets, and our prayers still come up before the Lord's presence as one corporate sound as we pray His will in His name.

Now I am no professional musician, but I do know that basically a symphony comprises several components: It requires a conductor, a score and an orchestra, meaning the musicians and their instruments.

In our symphony of prayer, the conductor is the Holy Spirit. The score is the will of God as revealed in His Word. The musicians are those brought together in the name of Jesus. With these components in place, the Holy Spirit lifts the baton of His authority and unites the playing of many different instruments.

I would like for you to think about prayer as taking your place in the orchestra and playing your instrument. You are not confined to one instrument, of course, although you probably have an affinity for a particular one. These instruments are praise, thanksgiving, worship, petition, intercession, supplication, command, commitment, dedication, persistence, blessing and cursing. This list is not exhaustive; there are more. But this will be sufficient to keep us busy! These instruments will help equip us to "pray in the Spirit on all occasions with all kinds of prayers and requests" (Ephesians 6:18, NIV).

Praise and Thanksgiving

I always like to begin times of prayer with these two instruments: praise and thanksgiving. Praise is offered to God for who He is and what He does in general. Thanksgiving is offered to God for what He has done for us in particular. Now, granted, if you are having an emergency—you are about to slide into another car ahead of you—you do not have time to do a lot of talking. But apart from that, it is a good principle to start with these two instruments.

Psalm 48:1 tells us: "Great is the LORD, and greatly to be praised." Praise is vocal. It is uttered. Praise should be offered in proportion to God's own Person. He is great—great in wisdom, great in power, great in His creative works, great in His redemptive acts, great in His dealings with us. Everything that God is and does is great. He should, therefore, be greatly praised. We never waste time when we are praising the Lord. Most of us do it far too little.

Thanksgiving is also vocal. It takes all the greatness that is universal about God and makes it specific for our particular cases. Listen to what Paul said: "Be anxious for nothing, but in everything by prayer and supplication, with thanksgiving, let your requests be made known to God" (Philippians 4:6).

As I understand it, thanksgiving and praise give us direct access to God. Psalm 100:4 gives these familiar words: "Enter His gates with thanksgiving, and His courts with praise. Give thanks to Him, bless His name" (NASB). The gate leads into the courts, the courts lead into His presence. You get through the gates with thanksgiving, and through the courts with praise. Then you are there.

Without these instruments we are something like the ten lepers who came to Jesus for help. They stood at a distance and cried out, "Lord, have mercy on us!" (see Luke 17:11–19). He did have mercy on them, but they never had access to Him. A lot—millions—of Christians pray like that. "Lord, help me. I need money. Heal me." But they are crying from a distance because they are not using a powerful means of access to God.

In that story of the lepers you will find that one of them returned to give thanks. When he did that, he had direct access to Jesus. The Bible says all ten of them were healed but only one was saved. By giving thanks he got spiritual as well as physical benefits.

I was speaking in Jerusalem one time when an old Christian came up to me. I mean old in every way: He was as old as I was and he had been in the Lord longer than I—a very respected man of God. I had been speaking on this subject and thought it was something everybody knows, but he said, "You caught me right between the eyes about coming into God's presence with praise and thanksgiving." He had been a Christian for fifty years and apparently had never understood this principle.

A beautiful phrase in Isaiah gives us another image of coming into God's presence. It is a prophetic description of the City of God—the place where God dwells, the home of God's people. Speaking of this beautiful place, Isaiah said, "You shall call your walls Salvation, and your gates Praise" (Isaiah 60:18).

The walls of this city are Salvation. That refers to God's provision and protection for His people. *Salvation* is the great, all-inclusive word for every benefit and every blessing that was purchased for us by the death of Jesus on the cross.

This city whose walls are Salvation also has gates. The book of Revelation tells us clearly that the only way into this glorious city is through the gate (see Revelation 21:25–27; 22:14). If we want to get into the city of Salvation, if we want to get into the presence of God, if we want to come into the enjoyment of all God's provision and protection and blessings for His people, we enter through the gate of Praise.

John Wesley wrote this in his journal: "I am persuaded that God does everything by prayer and nothing without it." And I would say Amen to that. Paul said, "In everything by prayer and supplication . . . let your requests be made known to God," but he added, "with thanksgiving" (Philippians 4:6). In other words, when you come to God with your requests, never fail to start by thanking Him.

There is a city in Northern Ireland called Bangor that my wife, Ruth, and I had a long connection with. In this city lived a group of monks who for more than one hundred years maintained unceasing thanksgiving and praise to God, 24 hours of every day, every week, every year. They were pretty tough, those old monks. If they thought they might fall asleep on the job, they would wade out into the river and stand up to their necks in water.

If you go there I think you will sense something different about that place. It is different from any other city. In fact, the city of Bangor is right next door to a city called Holywood. Bangor with its history of continuous praise also has a history of many visitations of God. Holywood, which is physically contiguous, never had a visitation until just recently.

Holywood, by the way, is called Holywood because it contains a grove that was sacred to Druidic worship. Until we discerned the reason why the Spirit of God never rested on Holywood, nothing happened there. When we understood that we had to break that satanic power over it, we experienced something of a release of God's Spirit in that place.

Put simply, then, you *praise* God for His greatness. You *thank* God for His goodness to you, for all that He has done for you. Giving thanks has a very important psychological function. It builds our faith. The more we stop and thank God for all that He has done for us, the easier it is for us to believe that He is going to do what we are going to ask next.

Also, it is good manners.

Worship

Worship is poorly understood in contemporary Christendom. Worship is not singing hymns or choruses; worship is not a declaration of God's attributes. Vocal expression has to do with praise and thanksgiving; worship has to do with attitude.

Most of the words translated "worship" both in the Old Testament and in the New describe primarily an attitude of the body. Different attitudes are represented by different words. One means to bend the head low. Another means to bend the upper part of the body forward and stretch out the hands. A third means to prostrate oneself face downward in the presence of the One whom one is worshiping. Thanksgiving and praise are vocal, meaning they come out of our mouths; worship is the attitude (or position of the body) in which we come. Now I do not mean to say that worship cannot be expressed vocally, but it is not worship if it is not an attitude of the body.

In the sixth chapter of Isaiah, the prophet described a vision of the throne of God. Above it he saw the seraphim, the burning fiery creatures that surround God's throne. He saw that each had six wings, and he saw how they used them.

With one pair of wings the seraphim covered their faces; with the second pair they covered their feet; with the third pair they flew. We understand from this picture that two pairs of wings are given to worship (indicated by covering their faces and feet) and the third pair to service (indicated by flying). This tells us that worship comes before service, and also that worship is twice as important as service.

Worship, in a sense, is covering your face and your body. It is bowing low, bending the head. Of course, this does not have to be solely a description of the physical body; we are talking about something in the spirit—the approach of our spirits to God. Jesus said, "The true worshipers will worship the Father in spirit and truth" (John 4:23).

This is represented in the Lord's Prayer: "In this manner, therefore, pray: Our Father in heaven" (Matthew 6:9). After we have first addressed God, the next thing we say is: "Hallowed be Your name. Your name is holy. It is a privilege even to use Your name. We do it with reverence; we do it in lowliness; we do it in awe and wonder and honor."

That is worship—a heart bowed low in God's presence.

73

Petition

The instrument that most people mean when they talk about "prayer" is petition, asking for physical and material needs to be met. But remember: Praying is not just thinking of anything we want and asking for it. Praying is discovering God's revealed purpose in Scripture, and then praying for the outworking of that purpose.

Look again at 1 John 5:14–15: "Now this is the confidence that we have in Him, that if we ask anything according to His will, He hears us. And if we know that He hears us, whatever we ask, we know that we have the petitions that we have asked of Him."

That is petition—asking for things. We looked at this verse in chapter 2 and learned that if we are asking according to His will, then He hears us. And if we know that He hears us, then we have what we ask for. If you are making a petition and you are praying in the will of God, you should walk away knowing you have received what you have asked for.

One of the great secrets of getting things from God is receiving. Lots of people ask but never receive. There is an old song that was sung to the tune of "In the cross, in the cross, be my glory ever." It goes:

> When you pray, when you pray,
> Do you pray believing?
> Do you pray the Bible way,
> Asking and receiving?

It is not just asking that is important, but asking and receiving. I have seen this many times. God touches someone with a healing touch, but the person does not receive it. One way *not* to receive an answer to a petition is to go on praying for it. Some people pray themselves into faith and then pray themselves out of faith.

Another Scripture is even more emphatic. Jesus was speaking about this very matter of petition when He said this: "Therefore I tell you, whatever you ask for in prayer, believe that you have received it, and it will be yours" (Mark 11:24, NIV). Some translations say, "Believe that you receive them," but that is not correct—or at least not literal. The New International Version is more accurate in this instance. "Believe that you *have* received it." When do you receive the things you ask for? When you pray.

Notice this, though: Receiving is not the same as having. Receiving is settling it; having is the experience that follows. The actual experience of having what we have prayed for may have to wait, but by faith we receive what we pray for when we pray. Say you have a financial need. You pray. You are in touch with God. You say, "God, we need two thousand dollars by Thursday." Then you say, "Thank You, God." You have received it. Nothing has changed in the circumstances, but you have received it. You will have it.

I sometimes define our stance in this intermediate state as "keeping the plug in." Let me give you an example. I first met Ruth in Jerusalem when she was virtually crippled. She had fallen while going down stairs and had seriously ruptured a disc. She spent most of her time lying in bed and was in continuous pain. In addition to her ruptured disc she had curvature of the spine, and the curvature was just at the point where the disc had ruptured, which made both of them worse.

God has given me special faith for people with back problems, and I went out of a sense of duty and prayed for her. I was not at the time, let me say, looking for a wife. That was an extra benefit!

After I had prayed I was a little disappointed that there was no immediate or dramatic improvement in Ruth's condition. But, thank God, she is a woman of faith. I told her, as I tell others, "Now you're plugged into God's supernatural power. Keep the plug in."

How do you do that? Basically, by thanking God. If you have made a petition regarding physical healing, for instance, you say, "Thank You, Lord. You touched me. Your power is at work in my body." Every time you feel a twinge of pain or you see a symptom, you say, "Thank You, Lord. Your supernatural power is at work in my body." And as you respond that way, the healing is completed.

Ruth had the faith and the guts to keep the plug in and just thank God continually for her healing. Her spine began to improve a little but not very much. In the meantime, she realized that she had never really considered what it meant to care for her body as the temple of the Holy Spirit. While she kept the plug in, she also began to care for her body with disciplines such as exercise.

A good many months later she was in a meeting when the spirit of rejoicing came over the people. She got up and began to dance, and as she was dancing before the Lord, not even thinking about her physical condition, her ruptured disc was healed instantly. But you see, she had the plug in all that time.

Years later, she had no ruptured disc and her spine was straight. It had never been straight since childhood. That is plugging into God's purpose—and keeping the plug in until you have the answer to your petition.

Do you see that in the matter of prayer it is not enough to have faith? You need faith and patience. Consider Abraham. God promised him a great multitude of descendants when he had no children. But Scripture says that "after [Abraham] had patiently endured, he obtained the promise" (Hebrews 6:15). How long did he wait? Twenty-five years. He was 99 years old before he had the promised son. Think of the endless times that he must have been tempted to doubt—to take the plug out.

Hebrews 10:36 tells us that we "have need of endurance, so that after [we] have done the will of God, [we] may receive the promise." In that gap between doing the will of God and receiving the promise you can do two things. You can keep the plug in or pull the plug out. If you pull the plug out you get nothing. If you keep the plug in you get everything.

What is God testing? Your perseverance.

Something that can help us in this process of keeping the plug in is learning to make the right confession—that is, declaring our faith boldly with our lips. I have found that there are certain ways to express your faith that have tremendous power—they release the power of God and they encourage us and strengthen us. Very often when I am praying in the morning or at the end of the day I make these simple confessions. Here, for instance, is a statement that concerns the body that I say several times a week:

> My body is the temple of the Holy Spirit: redeemed, cleansed and sanctified by the blood of Jesus. My members are instruments of righteousness yielded to God for His service and for His glory. The devil has no place in me, no power over me, no unsettled claims against me. All has been settled by the blood of Jesus. I overcome Satan by the blood of the Lamb and by the word of my testimony.

Another one of my favorites is a verse from 2 Corinthians 2:14: "But thanks be to God, who always leads us in triumphal procession in Christ and through us spreads everywhere the fragrance of the knowledge of him" (NIV). To me that is such a beautiful thought: If we walk in Christ's victory, out of that victory there is a fragrance that is wafted abroad by the Holy Spirit and blesses all those with whom we come in contact.

Let me give you a few more examples of things that I have petitioned God for. First and foremost, though, remember this: If you are going to petition God for something, always begin with thanksgiving. Never go straight into petition. And never use petition as a way to parade someone's faults before God. Sometimes we might see something that needs to be corrected in the life of a certain person. We may feel free to pray in a positive way for that correction, but we must make it a principle never to pray like that for a person until we have found something in that person's life or ministry to give thanks to God for.

Now suppose I would like to petition God for a certain aspect of the ministry in which I am involved. First I might thank God for the continuing expansion of our ministry. Then I could thank Him for all of the people who are involved in the work. I could then begin to petition God. I could ask for protection and direction in the continuing development and outreach of the radio ministry, and all who serve in that capacity. I would then persevere in that prayer by continuing to thank Him for hearing this prayer and believing that I have received these things.

Or suppose I am praying for Israel. I might begin with thanksgiving for God's covenant-keeping faithfulness to Israel and for His watching over His Word to them to see that it is fulfilled. Then I could go into a prayer of petition, asking God to raise up leadership in Israel inspired by biblical faith— leadership that is able to heal the long-standing divisions and guide Israel into her inheritance.

The prayer of petition is a prayer of receiving, which sometimes requires perseverance and endurance to hold on. As we will see in a moment, this is different from the prayer of persistence, which keeps on knocking at the door.

Intercession

Intercession is one of the highest arts of Christian life, one of the most difficult instruments to play. It requires a lot of practice, a lot of skill, a lot of maturity. *To intercede* means literally "to come in between." The intercessor is one who comes in between God and those for whom he is praying.

The Bible gives us examples of some extreme cases. One was the time that Abraham stood between the Lord and the wicked city of Sodom. Genesis 18 tells the story of the Lord and His two angels visiting Abraham's home—a remarkable picture of hospitality. Abraham offered them water to wash their feet; he killed a calf for their meal; he chatted with them in the shade of the terebinth trees.

Then the Lord began to unfold to Abraham His purpose in being there: He was going down into the wicked cities of Sodom and Gomorrah to investigate the situation and take appropriate action.

Now this concerned Abraham quite a bit because his nephew Lot, who was in a backslidden condition, was living in Sodom. Abraham knew that if judgment came upon Sodom, Lot and his family would be part of that judgment. At that point "the men [meaning the two angels] turned away from there and went toward Sodom, but Abraham still stood before the LORD" (Genesis 18:22).

That is the position of the intercessor. Abraham stood in front of the Lord and said, "Lord, hold on a moment. Don't go just yet. I have something to say to You." In a sense he held the Lord back. And then began a time of bargaining. Abraham asked if the Lord would spare the cities if He could find fifty righteous people, then forty and so on, until the Lord agreed to spare Sodom for the sake of ten righteous persons.

That is a tremendous revelation. I have tried to ascertain approximately the population of Sodom in the days of Abraham. Without going into the reasoning, I have come to believe that Sodom was a major city, and that its population could not have been fewer than ten thousand persons. If so, God said that for the sake of ten righteous persons He would spare a city of ten thousand who were wicked.

Now you do not have to be a mathematician to arrive at the proportion: It is one in a thousand. That is a very interesting—and biblical—proportion. Job 33:23 says: "If there is a messenger for him, a mediator, one among a thousand, to show man His uprightness. . . ." Ecclesiastes 7:28 says: "One man among a thousand I have found." It seems to be the proportion that indicates a person of outstanding righteousness.

In any event, we know from the conclusion of the story that the Lord did not find even ten righteous persons in the city, and He "rained brimstone and fire" (Genesis 19:24) on it.

Another biblical example of extreme intercession was the time when Moses prayed for Israel after the people had made the golden calf. In Exodus 32 we read that Moses had gone up Mount Sinai to commune with God and receive from Him the covenant. When he had been absent for some forty days, the people of Israel made a decision: "Moses is gone," they said. "We don't know what's become of him. We need a god. Come on, Aaron, make us a god." So Aaron took all their golden earrings, melted them together and made a molten calf. The people of Israel started to dance around it and worship it.

Moses was up on the top of the mountain with the Lord, when the Lord interrupted their conversation. He said, "Moses, you ought to know what's going on down at the foot of the mountain." There follows a conversation that is so intimate between these two it is in a sense amusing. Every time I read it I smile. Neither God nor Moses would accept responsibility for Israel. Each of them pushed the responsibility back on the other. I like the lyricism of the King James Version here:

> The LORD said unto Moses, Go, get thee down; for thy people, which thou broughtest out of the land of Egypt, have corrupted themselves: They have turned aside quickly out of the way which I commanded them: they have made them a molten calf, and have worshipped it. . . . The LORD said unto Moses, I have seen this people, and, behold, it is a stiffnecked people: Now therefore let me alone, that my wrath may wax hot against them, and that I may consume them: And I will make of thee a great nation.
>
> Exodus 32:7–10, KJV

I want you to notice that God would not act against His people in this manner unless Moses complied. He said, "Moses, get out of My way and let Me deal with these people. You see, Moses, I can wipe them out and still keep My promise to Abraham, Isaac and Jacob. I will simply establish you as the one through whom I rebuild this great nation."

Would that appeal to your ego? It would mine. Moses could have said, "Yes, God, blot out the people. After all, they have been nothing but a burden on me since I led them out of Egypt. Start again with me. I'll be the great ancestor of this people."

That is not what Moses did. "Moses besought the LORD his God, and said, LORD, why doth thy wrath wax hot against thy people, which thou hast brought forth out of the land of Egypt?" (verse 11, KJV). In other words, "Lord, they're not mine; they're Yours! I can't handle them! You are the One to deal with them."

Then this humble man of prayer went to work. He stated first that his supreme concern was for God's glory. He argued that since God had brought these people out of Egypt, the Egyptians would say that He had evil intentions against them all along. Next he reminded God of His promises and His covenant.

> Remember Abraham, Isaac, and Israel, thy servants, to whom thou swarest by thine own self, and saidst unto them, I will multiply your seed as the stars of heaven, and all this land that I have spoken of will I give unto your seed, and they shall inherit it for ever. And the LORD repented of the evil which he thought to do unto his people.
>
> Verses 13–14, KJV

Having stayed the Lord's hand, Moses went down to the bottom of the mountain, dealt with the people and then came up again.

> Moses returned unto the LORD and said, Oh, this people have sinned a great sin, and have made them gods of gold. Yet now, if thou wilt forgive their sin—; and if not, blot me, I pray thee, out of thy book which thou hast written.
>
> Verses 31–32, KJV

In this exchange we see Moses' heart of fervent prayer, supplication and intercession: "God, these people have sinned grievously. They deserve Your stroke. I ask that You have mercy on them. But if not, Lord, let their judgment come upon me."

Psalm 106 gives a divine commentary on this incident:

> They made a calf in Horeb, and worshipped the molten image. Thus they changed their glory into the similitude of an ox that eateth grass. They forgat God their saviour, which had done great things in Egypt; wondrous works in the land of Ham, and terrible things by the Red sea. Therefore he [God] said that he would destroy them, had not Moses his chosen stood before him in the breach, to turn away his wrath, lest he should destroy them.
>
> Verses 19–23, KJV

When someone's sin has caused a breach, the intercessor stands before God and says, "Lord, I'm stopping the gap. Your blow can't fall upon him unless it first falls upon me." This example also shows the position of the supplicant who calls out for mercy, as we will see in a moment.

This is not the only form of intercession, but it is the supreme. The intercessor is God-centered. He is not problem-focused; he is not focused on what man can or cannot do. He has a vision of what God can do. When no intercessor can be found among God's people, it is the supreme mark of failure in our responsibility to God and to our fellow man.

The story of Job praying for his family is another example.

> And his sons would go and feast in their houses, each on his appointed day, and would send and invite their three sisters to eat and drink with them. So it was, when the days of feasting had run their course, that Job would send and sanctify them, and he would rise early in the morning and offer burnt offerings according to the number of them all [that's seven

sons and three daughters—ten burnt offerings]. For Job said, "It may be that my sons have sinned and cursed God in their hearts." Thus Job did regularly.

Job 1:4–5

That is intercession. How far can we accept responsibility for other people's sins? I do not think that the human mind can give a final analysis. But to some extent we can accept responsibility for other people's sins by intercession. This is what Job did for his sons and his daughters. He said, "If by any chance they have sinned, I am offering this sacrifice." And he rose early in the morning to do it.

When I think of intercession corporately, I think of people meeting to offer sacrifice on behalf of the whole body, to stand as representatives before God and say, "We're here for our congregation. If anybody has sinned, Lord, we offer up sacrifice. If you want to speak to the body, Lord, they're not all here. But we are here."

You could say that Job did not get much for his sacrifices because all his sons and daughters were blotted out in one moment. But I want to point out to you something that to me is tremendously exciting—especially for those of us who have lost loved ones. If you read on, the end of the book says that after Job had stood the test, God gave him exactly double of everything he had before.

The Lord blessed the latter days of Job more than his beginning; for he had fourteen thousand sheep [previously he had seven thousand], six thousand camels [previously he had just three thousand], one thousand yoke of oxen [previously he had five hundred], and one thousand female donkeys [previously he had five hundred]. He also had seven sons and three daughters.

Job 42:12–13

God did not double the sons and daughters, however. He gave Job the same number. What is the message? Job had not lost his previous sons and daughters; they had gone before him. If you have ever lost a loved one or are ever going to lose a loved one, just bear that in mind. Job's sacrifices prevailed for his sons and daughters. God did not have to double the numbers because they were still there in the eternal.

If you are praying for your family—and most of us need to intercede for someone in our families—be encouraged. Get up early in the morning and offer the appropriate sacrifice. Trust God with the results.

When I was saved, I was the only member in my whole family that I knew of who was born again. My family were good people, but they were not that kind of people. I prayed for many, many years for my parents. I had the joy of leading my mother to the Lord when she was sick with Parkinson's disease. It was probably the last time she could really understand and respond. A miracle took place because when I asked her to pray, she lifted up her hands. First of all, she could not lift her hands and, second, she never would have lifted up her hands anyhow, believe me.

Once, not long after I was saved, I was lying in bed and I just began to sing or to chant in tongues. I had no idea what I was praying about, but the Lord gave me the interpretation. My prayer was, "Lord, save my father." It was such a blessing to me because I was not even thinking about my father at the moment; it was not in my conscious mind. I do have to trust the Lord that He did save my father. If He did, well, that is a miracle! My father was a good man, but he was not a religious man.

Let me give you one more example of intercession. This is a little picture from the gospel of Luke about the prophetess Anna, whose real name was Hannah. The English tend to drop the *H* off of some Hebrew words, which is a pity.

There was one, Anna, a prophetess, the daughter of Phanuel, of the tribe of Asher. She was of a great age, and had lived with a husband seven years from her virginity; and this woman was a widow of about eighty-four years, who did not depart from the temple, but served God with fastings and prayers night and day. And coming in that instant [when Jesus was being presented to the Lord] she gave thanks to the Lord, and spoke of Him to all those who looked for redemption in Jerusalem.

Luke 2:36–38

This has become a very vivid picture to me. That old precious lady never left the Temple night or day. She spent most of her time in fasting. What was she? She was an intercessor. Why was she in the Temple when she could have prayed in her own home? She was representing her people. She was there on behalf of Israel crying out to God for the redemption of Israel. God rewarded those many, many years of prayer by letting her see the Redeemer and recognize Him.

It is a kind of hidden life, in a way, the life of intercession. It is not very much in the public eye. But it moves the arm of God.

How about it? Are you willing to consider the responsibility of offering yourself to God as an intercessor? Here are four qualifications that I see in every scriptural intercessor. I think these are self-evident.

First of all, an intercessor must have an absolute conviction of God's righteousness, but he must be absolutely convinced also that God will judge the wicked. There is no room for a kind of milk-and-water religion that thinks God is too kind to judge sin. Anybody who thinks like that cannot qualify to be an intercessor. An intercessor has to have a crystal-clear vision of the absolute justice and inevitability of God's justice.

Second, he has to have a deep concern for God's glory. This, remember, is why Moses twice turned down the offer to be the ancestor of the greatest people on earth. He said, "God, that would not be for Your glory. What would the Egyptians say about Your character?"

Third, I believe such a person must have an intimate acquaintance with God. An intercessor is a person who can stand before God and talk to Him with the utmost frankness—and yet reverence.

And finally, to be an intercessor takes holy boldness. You must be willing to risk your life. Aaron was this kind of intercessor when he took the incense and stood between the plague God had sent and the people God intended to destroy by it (see Numbers 16:42–48). As an intercessor you say, "I may run the risk of death, but I am going to stand here."

Supplication

The next instrument in the symphony of prayer is supplication. *Supplication* is a complicated word for some people. When you are supplicating or you are a supplicant, there is only one thing you ask for: mercy. It is often tied to intercession.

Let's look at two passages that describe this. Zechariah 12:10 is a prophecy directed at Israel. The Lord was speaking and He said: "I will pour on the house of David and on the inhabitants of Jerusalem the Spirit of grace and supplication."

Notice the order: first grace, then supplication. If you say, "God, I want to come before You in supplication," God will say, "If I don't give you the grace, you can't do it." Actually no prayer of any value can be offered to God without His grace. If it does not initiate in the grace of God it is worthless.

The next part of that verse in Zechariah 12 reads: "Then they will look on Me whom they pierced. Yes, they will mourn for Him as one mourns for his only son, and grieve for Him as one grieves for a firstborn."

This verse describes the turning point of God's dealings with Israel. It is the point at which they come to repentance and acknowledgment of the Messiah, and it is brought about by the Spirit of grace and supplication.

God is so logical. You see, when the Father sent Jesus to Israel, Israel as a nation rejected Him. God did not reject His people, though; He sent them the Holy Spirit. But then when they rejected the Holy Spirit, there was nothing more that He could do. That was the ultimate decision against God. Jesus said, "You can blaspheme against the Son and be forgiven, but not against the Spirit" (see Matthew 12:31).

Now I mention this because we are seeing the situation in Israel start to change. There is a process of restoration, and it is moving in reverse order. A lot of Christians think the Jewish people will first be confronted with Jesus. Oh, no! They will first be moved on by the Holy Spirit, and the Holy Spirit will reveal Jesus to them. This process has already begun. It is actually quite comical to watch, because God is sneaking up on their blind side! I have talked to many Jewish people in this situation. It takes a certain amount of wisdom to know at what point to stop talking and leave it to the Holy Spirit to finish.

Hebrews 4 gives another beautiful picture of supplication, one we have already viewed. Hebrews, of course, was written to Jewish believers. "Let us therefore come boldly to the throne of grace, that we may obtain mercy and find grace to help in time of need" (Hebrews 4:16).

God sits upon a throne, but it is a throne of grace. And what do we come for? *To obtain mercy and find grace to help in time of need.* If you tend to feel overwhelmed by a particularly serious situation and think that there is nothing left to do, then hear what God says: "The time of need is the time to come."

I am convinced that the only people who fail to receive mercy and grace are the people who do not come to the throne. We do not see our own need. We are blinded by self-righteousness and religiosity, but if we could earn God's mercy we would not need it. As we come, we receive.

Command

The instrument of command takes us into a different area—it speaks with aggression and authority.

Joshua 10 is a good place to start. This Scripture describes a scene in the middle of a battle. The Israelites were defeating their enemies, but it was getting dark. If night fell they would not be able to finish the job off.

> Then Joshua spoke to the LORD [notice he began by speaking to the Lord] in the day when the LORD delivered up the Amorites before the children of Israel, and he [Joshua] said in the sight of Israel: "Sun, stand still over Gibeon; and Moon, in the Valley of Aijalon." So the sun stood still, and the moon stopped, till the people had revenge upon their enemies. Is this not written in the Book of Jasher? So the sun stood still in the midst of heaven, and did not hasten to go down for about a whole day. And there has been no day like that, before it or after it, that the LORD heeded the voice of a man.
>
> Verses 12–14

That is the prayer of command addressed to the Lord. We can tell situations and circumstances how to behave—but we will not have results unless we have first contacted the Lord, and, second, received the anointing, the release for such a prayer.

A New Testament example is the incident of the fig tree that Jesus cursed. There are two gospel accounts of this story. Here is the first.

> Now in the morning, as He returned to the city, He was hungry. And seeing a fig tree by the road, He came to it and found nothing on it but leaves, and said to it, "Let no fruit grow on you ever again." Immediately the fig tree withered away [within 24 hours, as we discover in the other gospel story]. And when the disciples saw it, they marveled, saying, "How did the fig tree wither away so soon?" So Jesus answered and said to them, "Assuredly, I say to you, If you have faith and do not doubt, you will not only do what was done to the fig tree, but also if you say to this mountain, 'Be removed and be cast into the sea,' it will be done. And whatever things you ask in prayer, believing, you will receive."
>
> Matthew 21:18–22

Notice there are two ways of using words of command that are brought out there. One way is toward things on behalf of God; the other way is toward God on behalf of things. Jesus did not *pray about* the fig tree. He also did not *pray to* the fig tree, which would have been idolatry. He *spoke to* the fig tree on behalf of God. This was not prayer. He simply told the fig tree what to do, and the fig tree did it.

According to the leading of the Holy Spirit, then, we may either speak to the thing on behalf of God (as Jesus did to the fig tree), or speak to God on behalf of a thing, which is what we normally call prayer.

The same incident is recorded in Mark 11, but there is one further truth revealed by Jesus, which really is the key to understanding it all.

> Now in the morning, as they passed by, they saw the fig tree dried up from the roots. And Peter, remembering, said to Him, "Rabbi, look! The fig tree which You cursed has withered away." So Jesus answered and said to them, "Have faith in God."
>
> Mark 11:20–22

The literal translation is "Have the faith of God." The prayer of command is God's faith expressed in utterances; thus, it is just as authoritative as if God Himself had spoken them. In a certain sense, because these words are being breathed forth by the Spirit of God, they are God-given utterances.

Scripture affirms that this word of command is for us to employ today.

> The effective, fervent prayer of a righteous man avails much. Elijah was a man with a nature like ours, and he prayed earnestly that it would not rain; and it did not rain on the land for three years and six months. And he prayed again, and the heaven gave rain, and the earth produced its fruit.
>
> James 5:16–18

In other words, through fervent prayer you and I can do the same. That same power is available to us.

Here are two modern-day examples. You may never have heard of a brother named Howard Carter. His story goes way back into the early days of the Pentecostal movement in Britain. He was an author and founded England's first Pentecostal Bible school in London.

In World War I, Howard was a conscientious objector and wound up in prison because of it. The prison was a damp, leaky place. He was lying in his bed one day and a little stream of water was trickling down from the ceiling and splashing over him. He pointed his finger at it and said, "I command you to go back, in the name of Jesus." And it did.

Here is another story. In Zambia, a teenage African girl was bicycling to the place where we were holding a meeting. They have vast anthills in Zambia—twenty or thirty feet high—and they are home to snakes. As she approached an anthill, a big black cobra came out of its hole toward her. She came to a stop on her bicycle, trembling terribly. But then the Spirit of God came upon her, and she said, "In the name of the Lord Jesus Christ, go back into your hole."

The cobra stopped and turned its head toward the hole, but it remained motionless. She spoke again: "No, I said go back into your hole." At that, it turned around and went right back in. When she got to our meeting place she was still trembling. In that command God's strength was made perfect in weakness.

This instrument of prayer is particularly appropriate to use when we follow Jesus' directive to cast out demons (see Mark 16:17).

Commitment

The next instrument, the prayer of commitment, is very important to understand. As with the prayer of petition, sometimes the way to pray about a thing is to stop praying about it.

Here is a prayer of commitment. You will recognize that the first part of this verse from the Psalms was quoted by Jesus on the cross: "Into Your hand I commit my spirit; You have redeemed me, O LORD God of truth" (Psalm 31:5). There are times when our best decision is to commit our situations to the Lord and simply take our hands off. I remember the first time I preached in Denmark. It was in 1947 and I was there on my own. Lydia, my first wife, was still in Jerusalem. I was being introduced everywhere as her husband, and because of her somewhat prestigious position and the raised eyebrows regarding her born-again experience, it was important that the Danish people thought well of me for her sake.

When I met the Dane who was to be my interpreter I realized that he did not understand 50 percent of what I said to him. I could not imagine what I was to do in that situation; I thought, *This is hopeless.* So in despair I said, "Lord, into Your hands I commit my spirit."

I have no idea how it happened, but we had a tremendous meeting. I have never known if he actually interpreted what I said or if he spoke what he wanted to say, but the results were wonderful. I had to take my hands off the situation. There was nothing more I could do.

Psalm 37:5, a familiar verse, gives this encouragement: "Commit your way to the LORD, trust also in Him, and He shall bring it to pass." The Hebrew actually says, *Roll your way on the Lord.* This became clear to me when I was working with students in East Africa. Sometimes we would run out of rice and have nothing for supper. I would then drive down to the local town in my little Morris Traveler station wagon and get two sacks of rice. They weighed two hundred and twenty pounds each, as I recall.

Now one of the things we wrestled with at our school in Africa was the notion that as soon as the young people started to get educated they thought it was demeaning to do physical work. I wanted to demonstrate to them that that was not so. So I would drive up to the kitchen with the bags of rice, haul one of the sacks onto my back and carry it into the kitchen. Interestingly, it is actually easier to get something that heavy on than it is to get it off. I learned the secret: Roll it off.

That is what the Lord is saying in this verse. When your way becomes too heavy for you and you can no longer handle it, just roll it off onto the Lord and He will take care of it. Commitment is an act. And once you commit, you should not go back and see if it is working. You trust. It is like taking money to the bank and making a deposit. Once you get your receipt, you would not think of walking back thirty minutes later to see if the bank knows what to do with your money. You have committed it to the bank. If you commit something to the Lord, leave it.

I remember years back in Ireland when a little six-year-old boy, a cousin of mine, planted some potatoes. He was so anxious to see if the potatoes were growing, he kept going back and digging them up. He never got any potatoes. A lot of Christians are like that. They plant their potatoes and then they dig them up to see if they are growing. If you commit, then you have to trust. And while you trust, the Lord is taking care of it.

Dedication

The next prayer instrument is dedication. This is similar to the prayer of commitment. In both cases we give the object of our prayer to the Lord, but in dedication, the thing we are offering is ourselves. In a prayer of dedication we set ourselves apart, choosing to consecrate or sanctify ourselves for the particular work or calling that God has placed on our lives.

We find an example of this in John 17:19, which is part of what we call the High Priestly Prayer of Jesus. He was speaking about His relationship to His disciples and to the Father. He said, "For their sakes I sanctify Myself, that they also may be sanctified by the truth." Like Jesus, if we choose to set ourselves apart to God, then we belong to God. We are in His hands and are not allowed to do what we want.

Jesus said in John 10:36 that the Father had sanctified Him and sent Him into the world. How did the Father sanctify Jesus? He did not make Him holy, of course, because He was already holy. Rather He set Him apart to a work that no one else could do. So Jesus at this point was saying, "I sanctify Myself. I set Myself apart to the work for which God has already set Me apart."

Always with sanctification the initiative is with God. You cannot sanctify yourself for something for which God has not sanctified you. You have to find out what God has set you apart for, and then you set yourself apart to do it, responding with your own will. It is an amazing thing that multitudes of born-again Christians have never discovered this. God has set us apart, but it does not become effective until we set ourselves apart.

You do not have to do this; it is voluntary. But remember that the Bible does not give you permission to make a vow and then ask to change it back.

Persistence

Jesus taught His disciples to take up the prayer instrument of persistence.

95

And He said to them, "Which of you shall have a friend, and go to him at midnight and say to him, 'Friend, lend me three loaves; for a friend of mine has come to me on his journey, and I have nothing to set before him'; and he will answer from within and say, 'Do not trouble me; the door is now shut, and my children are with me in bed; I cannot rise and give to you'? I say to you, though he will not rise and give to him because he is his friend, yet because of his persistence he will rise and give him as many as he needs."

Luke 11:5–8

In other words, you keep on knocking, letting your friend know he is not going to get any sleep that night until he gets up and gives you the bread. Jesus commended that kind of persistence:

So I say to you, ask [literally, keep on asking], and it will be given to you; seek [and keep on seeking], and you will find; knock [and keep on knocking], and it will be opened to you. For everyone who asks [and keeps on asking] receives, and he who seeks [and keeps on seeking] finds, and to him who knocks [and keeps on knocking] it will be opened.

Verses 9–10

This is quite different from the prayer of petition, which receives the thing being prayed for even though it often requires perseverance to "keep the plug in." In that case, you pray; you receive; you say, "Thank You, Lord." That is it. In this kind of persistent prayer you go on knocking, knocking, knocking, knocking, continuing to ask for the thing you desire until the door is opened.

I knew of a South African missionary who wanted to get into Mozambique to open a Protestant mission. At that time the country was under Portuguese government and almost exclusively Catholic. She went to the Mozambique Council and asked for their permission. She was refused. She went again. She was refused. She went again. She was refused. Do you know how many times she went? Thirty-three times, and the thirty-third time she got permission. That is asking and keeping on asking!

Acts 12 gives us an example of persistent prayer by the early Church. King Herod had the apostle James, the brother of John, executed. Then he proceeded to arrest Peter and hold him for execution immediately after the Passover. At this point the Church in Jerusalem betook themselves to earnest, persistent prayer on Peter's behalf. Sometimes God will not work merely through the prayer of an individual. It takes the corporate prayer of a group of committed believers praying together.

"So Peter was kept in prison, but the church was earnestly praying to God for him" (Acts 12:5, NIV). Notice that word *but*. That *but* changed the course of events. The united corporate prayer of the Church opened the way for the intervention of an angel who came from God and delivered Peter out of the prison.

In this way, the prayers of the Church for Peter were answered, but it still remained for God to deal with King Herod.

In the closing verses of Acts 12, Luke described Herod, arrayed in his royal apparel, making a speech to the people of Tyre and Sidon. At the end of his oration the people applauded, shouting, "This is the voice of a god, not of a man" (verse 22, NIV). Puffed up with conceit at his own achievement, Herod accepted the applause. The record concludes that immediately an angel of the Lord struck Herod down because he did not give God the glory. "And he was eaten by worms and died" (verse 23, NIV).

See again the outworking of the persistent prayer of the Church. Everything that had been resisting the word and the purpose of God was overthrown, and Herod died a miserable, agonizing and shameful death. Notice that it was the intervention of an angel that terminated the career of Herod. What brought the intervention of the angel twice in this story? The prayer of the Church.

So we ask ourselves in light of all that, Who was really ruling? Was it Herod or the Church? The answer is Herod sat on the throne, but the Church ruled by, in this case, persistent prayer.

If you really believe you are going to get it, you will not stop. The only way you can lose is by giving up.

Since many prayers of persistence—and petition as well—involve the need for some aspect of healing, I want to mention here the difference between the working out of miracles and healings, for the two are distinct. Miracles actually go beyond healings.

Here is an example that has occurred more than once in my ministry. If a person has a condition called *otitis media*, which is inflammation of the middle ear, you can pray for it and it can be healed. But if a person has had the middle ear removed by surgery, you cannot heal a middle ear that is not there. A miracle, however, can restore a middle ear.

I remember two different occasions in which that happened. Once a man came up to me and said, "Pray for my ear." Thank God I did not ask him what was the matter with his ear. So I prayed. A few days later he came back and said, "I got healed."

I said, "What did you get healed of?"

He said, "I had no middle ear and now I've got one. I went to the doctor, he checked and I have a normal ear." That is a miracle. It goes beyond healing.

The difference also is this: Miracles are often instantaneous and often visible, whereas healings are often invisible and gradual. Some people come to get healed, and if they do not get a miracle they think nothing has happened. But it may be that they are receiving a healing. This is very important to understand because if you are receiving a healing, a lot will depend on how you respond.

Suppose you come up to be prayed for and God touches you, but you do not get a complete healing. If you walk away and say, "Nothing happened," what you have done is ensure that nothing more will happen.

A miracle is usually released by a simple act of faith. If you want to study a man who had a lot of miracles, look at the prophet Elisha. Almost every miracle that he performed was released by a rather ridiculous act of faith. For instance, there was a spring outside Jericho the water of which was corrupt. He took a vessel of salt, threw the salt into the spring and said, "Thus says the LORD: 'I have healed this water.'" Well, everybody knows that salt does not heal water. But you can go to that spring today, more than two thousand years later, and it is still healed. The salt did not heal the spring, but the little act of faith released God's miracle power into it (see 2 Kings 2:19–22).

Blessing

The last two prayers in our symphony are blessing and cursing. Here is a biblical prayer of blessing that will likely be familiar to you.

"Speak to Aaron and his sons, saying, 'This is the way you shall bless the children of Israel. Say to them: "The LORD bless you and keep you; the LORD make His face shine upon you, and be gracious to you; the LORD lift up His countenance upon you, and give you peace."' "

Numbers 6:23–26

Here are six blessings that you can pray for someone you want to bless: (1) The Lord bless you, (2) keep you, (3) make His face shine upon you, (4) be gracious to you, (5) lift up His countenance upon you and (6) give you peace. Whenever I read these blessings I kept thinking that six was not a perfect number; *there has to be something more.* God showed me this in the next verse: "So they shall put My name on the children of Israel, and I will bless them" (verse 27). That is the seventh blessing. Putting His name on them makes them complete.

Parents, that is how you can bless your children—you can put the name of the Lord upon them every day when they go to school or about their various activities, and He will keep them. What a privilege it is to be able to bless!

Cursing

The other side of blessing is cursing. Most Christians are not aware that we are also charged to curse. But let me say initially that this is not a license to bring destruction wherever you choose.

Let's return to the story in Matthew 21 of Jesus walking past the fig tree that had no fruit on it, only leaves. A lot of plans and programs and other things we see today look as though they might have fruit, but there is none when you look closer. Jesus was not indifferent about this. He did not say, "Well, nothing there." He said, "Let no one ever eat fruit from you again." The next morning, as we have noted, when they passed by the fig tree it was withered from the roots. The disciples were impressed, and this is what Jesus said to them:

> So Jesus answered and said to them, "Assuredly, I say to you, if you have faith and do not doubt, you will not only do what was done to the fig tree, but also if you say to this mountain, 'Be removed and be cast into the sea,' it will be done."
>
> Matthew 21:21

Now we all focus on removing the mountain, but Jesus said we can also do what was done to the fig tree: It was cursed.

I was part of the leadership team of a church in downtown Chicago in the late 1960s. The church was on a corner and stood wall to wall with a liquor store. That store was a wicked place—a center of prostitution and drugs as well as drunkenness.

One evening we were having a prayer meeting in the church and I was on the platform. Something came over me and I stood up and said, "Lord, I curse that liquor store in the name of Jesus." I then forgot about it.

That was in October. Just before Christmastime Lydia and I got a phone call at four in the morning. A dear lady from the church was on the line and said, "Brother Prince, the church is burning!" Now at that time the temperature outside was about twenty degrees below zero. I must say that Lydia and I were not strongly motivated to go stand outside! Rather reluctantly we got out of bed and climbed into the car and drove down.

We could see the flames two or three blocks away. When we got there, however, we discovered that the church was not burning—it was the liquor store. The church was not out of danger, however: The wind off Lake Michigan was blowing the flames directly toward it. But, as we stood there shivering, the wind direction changed one hundred and eighty degrees and blew the flames away from the church.

The church suffered no damage at all except minimal smoke damage, but the liquor store was demolished. The Chicago fire chief said to the elder of the church, "You must have a special relationship with the Man upstairs." Well, I knew why that liquor store burned down: I had cursed it. And I tell you it did not make me feel proud. It scared me. I knew that I had better think about what I said from then on.

But I think that if the Spirit of God prompts you to use this kind of prayer, it can further the purposes of God. Jesus was never indifferent. He was never neutral. He was either for or against and He expected everybody to be like Him.

Praying in Faith

Jesus said, "Man ought to persist in prayer and not to faint" (see Luke 18:1–8). I think Ruth and I discovered that this is one of the great tests of fitness for taking our places in His symphony. Christian character involves persistence in prayer. It is not going to God with a shopping list. That is hardly praying at all. Remember that Jesus said your Father knows what you need before you ask Him (see Matthew 6:8). You do not have to tell God what you need. What is important is that you get into such a relationship with God that when you do tell Him what you need, you know you are going to get it.

There are some things that I have been praying for ten years. They have not come yet. When that happens, you discover whether you are praying in faith or unbelief. If you are praying in unbelief, you probably say, "I have been praying for ten years and nothing has happened." But if you are praying in faith you say, "The answer is ten years nearer than when I started praying."

I hope this has created in you a desire to learn to play the different instruments. It is a wonderful thing to be part of this divine symphony of prayer. As you pray in harmony with others—under the baton of the Holy Spirit in accordance with the will of God as revealed in His Word—Jesus said that your prayers will be answered. Now let's learn more about how to know God's will for our prayers.

5

HOW TO DISCOVER GOD'S WILL

The word of God is living and powerful, and sharper than
any two-edged sword.

Hebrews 4:12

If you were to ask people "Whom do you consider to be
the most influential kinds of persons on earth?" I suppose
they might give various answers. Probably their minds
would turn to political leaders. Or perhaps scientists or military commanders.

I do not believe that these groups are the really influential
people. As I understand it, the most influential people on
earth today are those who know how to get their prayers
answered. This is because they can release the omnipotence
of God into situations, which goes far beyond anything that
the wisest or most powerful human being can do. I believe
that any dramatic changes for good in our world—take, for
instance, the overthrow of the Iron Curtain, or the release

of political liberty inside the Soviet Union—are not the decision of politicians; they are results of the prayers of God's people—the Kingdom of priests.

If that amount of authority has been committed to us as believers in Jesus Christ, we are really negligent if we do not appreciate and make use of it. As a Kingdom of priests, it is our mandate to rule the earth. We can change the course of history, and it centers on knowing God's will.

"In This Manner Pray"

If we turn to the Sermon on the Mount, we come to the portion of Scripture in Matthew 6 that is familiarly known to Christians around the earth as the Lord's Prayer. When Jesus said, "In this manner, therefore, pray," I do not believe that He meant by this that we always must use precisely the words that follow—although they are beautiful words. Rather, I believe He set forth a concise and yet complete pattern of the way we ought to pray.

Let's return to verses 9–10 and discover there the means of effective praying: "Our Father in heaven, hallowed be Your name. Your kingdom come. Your will be done on earth as it is in heaven." These words hold the key to finding God's will. I hope I can put this key into your hands and that it will help you unlock the omnipotence of God.

Our Father in Heaven

First of all, we address God as Father: our Father in heaven. That makes all the difference. We are not praying to a remote or unknown deity or some impersonal force. We are praying to a Person who has made Himself our Father through Jesus Christ.

You see, the mechanistic view of the universe—the idea that it is just the result of a series of material explosions—leaves a person very lonely, lost in the vastness of a universe that he does not understand and cannot control. When I think of this topic I always think of a friend of mine, a well-known Catholic charismatic speaker, who told me years back about a time when he was in one of the slums of a big city of the United States. It was late in the evening; it was getting dark. A cold wind was causing dust to swirl up around him. He was standing on the corner of the street, and he felt lonely and weak. Then it came to him to speak one word, addressing it to God, and he repeated again and again: "Father, Father, Father." The more he repeated the word *Father*, the stronger and more secure he felt. Simply reinforcing his relationship to Almighty God as his Father changed his outlook on the situation at that moment.

As a young man I had studied for a good many years the various theories about the origin of the universe. I never could find one that satisfied me intellectually. I started to read the Bible in desperation, thinking that at the very least it could not be any sillier than some of the other theories I had heard. I did not believe that it was divinely inspired or unique; I planned to treat it like any other book, starting at the beginning and reading to the end.

I made that decision in 1940 when I went into the army. I was called from a position as a professor of philosophy at Cambridge University into the British Forces in World War II, and I took a Bible along with me, planning to read it through while I was in the army. I had plenty of time because, not by my choice, I spent the next five and a half years in that occupation. I always recall the impact this made the first night I was in the barrack room with 24 other new recruits. I did not think anything about it. I just sat down and opened up the Bible.

The other soldiers began to look at me, and when they realized I was reading the Bible an uneasy hush fell on the whole barrack room. I could not believe that one book would have that much effect! I think what baffled them the most was the fact that I did not live the least bit like people who regularly read the Bible.

Through reading the Bible, however, I met the Author. And once I met the Author the book made the most wonderful sense to me. I found there the answers that I had not found in philosophy. I found a description of the beginning of things that explained me to myself. When I read the story of the creation of man in Genesis 1–3, I understood what was going on inside me.

See, my favorite philosopher, whom I studied extensively, was Plato. I read in the Greek language every word he ever wrote. Plato pictured the human soul like a chariot drawn by two horses—one black and one white. The white horse was always trying to go upward; the black horse was always pulling the chariot downward. I felt that his picture was true to my experience.

When I read the Genesis account I realized that man comes from two sources. He is from the dust of the earth below, but he is also from the breath of Almighty God above. I saw in every one of us something of a tension between what comes from above and what comes from the earth. But God shows us in His Word how to resolve that tension and bring our lives into harmony.

I had a totally different view of the universe from that time onward. When I met the God of the Bible, I came to understand that there was a Father and that the real power behind everything is His love. The one unexplained fact in the universe is the love of God. The Bible tells us God loves us, but it never tells us why. We just have to receive it; we will never understand it. Why God should love us passes our comprehension. But the good news is He really does.

Jesus said that when we start to pray to God, the first word we use is *Father*. In the English translation it comes out *our Father*, but in the Greek *Father* comes first and then *our*. If we know God as Father through Jesus Christ, the first thing we do when we pray is approach Him as Father. The word *our* is important because most of us are extremely self-centered. When we pray we tend to say, "Lord, bless me, help me, heal me." Jesus reminded us, "You are not the only child God has. He has a lot of other children and they are all important to Him. Care for your brothers and sisters."

Hallowed Be Your Name

The next phrase, *hallowed be Your name*, expresses an attitude of reverence, of worship. After we have acknowledged God as Father, we need to adopt an attitude of reverence. I have to say that in many sections of the Church today, the approach of reverence to Almighty God is sadly lacking. God does not want us terrified, but He does want us reverent. Something happens in our spirit when we let that attitude of reverence express itself in our prayers.

Your Kingdom Come

Next we come to the first two petitions: "Your kingdom come" and then "Your will be done on earth as it is in heaven." Notice that we do not begin by praying for what we need. That follows: "Give us this day our daily bread, and forgive us our trespasses." But that is not where we start. We start with God's purposes—what is important to God.

You see, through the Fall man was shut up in a little prison called self. Natural man is self-centered; his life focuses on himself. *How can I get what I want? Who's going to help me? What do I get out of this?* That is a prison.

Through the new birth and through the grace of God we can be released from that prison of self-centeredness and enter into a relationship with Him in which what God wants is more important than what we want. When you pray that way you are beginning to grow wings. You can move above the natural level.

So the first thing we are directed to say is: "Your kingdom come." That is tremendously important because what we are doing is aligning ourselves with what God wants done in the earth. God's ultimate purpose in this age is actually simple. The details may be complicated, but the essential plan of God is this: to establish His Kingdom on earth. That is God's first priority. All through the history of this age from the time that Jesus died and rose again until now, God's priority has never changed. Millions and millions of Christians pray the Lord's Prayer every day and never realize what they are praying for. When we say "Your Kingdom come," we are asking Him to do what He said He will do.

Ultimately the only possible solution to the needs of humanity is the establishment of God's Kingdom. We hear a lot today about a social gospel, meaning that we need to care for man's physical and material needs. All Christians should be concerned with the physical and material needs of our fellow human beings. I believe that is the expression of love. If you love people you will be concerned about their needs. But I do not believe that it is in our path to meet the needs of humanity as a whole.

The Church has been here nearly two thousand years and the needs in many cases are greater now than they have ever been at any time in human history. Twenty-five thousand children under the age of five die every week on the earth today, mainly of malnutrition and unsanitary conditions. And yet, if all the money that was spent by the nations on military armaments were made available, it would be abundant to establish hospitals, clinics and safe water supplies in every nation on earth. The problem is not the availability of resources; the problem is that human greed along with fear and hate cause the resources to be misdirected.

Now do not misunderstand me; I am not preaching pacifism. I am just pointing out that the root of the problem is in human nature. Man by himself or the Church by herself is never going to resolve the material and practical needs of humanity. Only one thing can do that: the establishment of God's Kingdom on earth.

I claim to be a practical person. I do not want to be just a visionary or a dreamer. I tell people that the Holy Spirit is the most practical Person on the earth today. If a thing is not practical, it is not spiritual. The establishment of God's Kingdom is the only practical solution to human need. The people who preach what is called a social gospel are presenting a dream. Their motives may be good, but to suggest that by merely focusing on man's material needs we can resolve them is not true. There is only one hope for humanity.

I have traveled widely and have been to a lot of places where people are desperately poor, in need and in ignorance. It is possible that most Christians have only a faint picture of the cries of humanity in many, many nations across the earth. The needs are not being met. In many cases poverty, deprivation and hunger are increasing.

There is a solution: God's solution. God is a great realist, and His love for humanity causes Him to make priority number one the meeting of humanity's needs through the establishment of Christ's Kingdom on earth.

How the Kingdom Is Established

Now we need to have a little clarity about the way the Kingdom is established. Paul defined the Kingdom in its essential nature: "The kingdom of God is not eating and drinking, but righteousness and peace and joy in the Holy Spirit" (Romans 14:17).

Righteousness comes first. Without true righteousness there will never be true peace. The world today talks a great deal about peace. Many sections of the Church are praying for peace. That is a good prayer, but bear in mind that without righteousness peace will never come. God says twice through the prophet Isaiah that there is no peace for the wicked (see Isaiah 48:22; 57:21).

I have met many Christians who want peace and joy, but often I have found they have omitted the fact that peace and joy come only as the results of righteousness. Righteousness is the first expression of the Kingdom. Any attempt to achieve peace without it is doomed to frustration.

My understanding of biblical prophecy is that there will come an Antichrist, a satanically inspired ruler. He will promise peace and will seem for a brief moment to achieve it. But Paul prophesied this: "When they say, 'Peace and safety!' then sudden destruction comes upon them [without warning]" (1 Thessalonians 5:3). Only the power of the Holy Spirit can impart righteousness, peace and joy in their true nature.

The first way that the Kingdom comes is inwardly. Jesus told the Pharisees of His day that the Kingdom does not

112

come by watching and waiting for it externally. He said that the Kingdom of God is within you or in your midst (see Luke 17:21).

There is no kingdom without a king. When any king comes in, he brings his kingdom with him. Every true believer who makes Jesus King of his life, therefore, can have an individual experience of the Kingdom. That means displacing "self" from the throne of one's heart and placing Jesus on that throne. Anyone who does that finds that the Kingdom of God sets in with righteousness, peace and joy.

But I believe there is also a corporate expression of the Kingdom. It is in the true community of believers, which is called the Church. This is the fellowship of those who have made Jesus King in their own hearts and lives and relate to one another on that basis.

It is the responsibility of the Church in any place to model the Kingdom of God, that by our attitudes and our relationships and the way we live we challenge the world with a glimpse of the Kingdom. People should be able to look at the Church and say, "So that's what the Kingdom of God is like." They should see in her righteousness, peace and joy in the Holy Spirit. I tell you that where the Church demonstrates these things, the hearts of men and women are nearly always open to the truth of the Gospel. If the world does not see the Kingdom in the Church, it will probably not believe our message.

Let me suggest one important way in which we can model the Kingdom, and it is not without controversy. The fact of the matter is that truth today is controversial. Isaiah wrote about a time when truth falls in the street and righteousness cannot enter. We are not far from a time like that in many parts of human society.

But here is one way to model our message. Paul said this to Christian married couples: "Husbands, love your wives, just as Christ also loved the church" (Ephesians 5:25). I tell husbands, "That is not a recommendation; that is a commandment. You are commanded to love your wife. Furthermore, it will do you a lot of good when you do it." The other side of it is this: "Therefore, just as the church is subject to Christ, so let the wives be to their own husbands in everything" (Ephesians 5:24).

When the world looks at Christian married couples, it should say, "I understand that the way that man loves his wife is the way Christ loved the Church. And the way that woman relates to her husband is the way the Church relates to Christ." A committed Christian couple can be a message to the world. This is what the Kingdom of God is like.

If there is one place that the Kingdom should be demonstrated first and foremost, it is in the believer's family. And if there is one place that Satan is attacking today, it is the family. The family was designed by God to represent the Kingdom, and Satan wants to blur, obscure and eliminate the message of the Kingdom. He is afraid of the Kingdom because wherever the Kingdom is established, his power has come to an end.

Ultimately the King Comes

The Kingdom can come invisibly—both in the individual hearts of believers and in the corporate fellowship of the true Church. But that is not the ultimate. The ultimate is the visible establishment of God's Kingdom. And just as the invisible Kingdom requires a King, so does the visible Kingdom. Only when the King Himself has returned visibly and in Person can the true Kingdom of God be established on earth. Personally, I have to say I feel it presumptuous for the Church to suggest that we can do the job and finish it off without Jesus. The Bible says that we should be eagerly longing for His appearing.

A friend of mine who is a preacher has a rather droll way of expressing himself. He said that when Jesus returns, the Church should do something more than say, "Nice to have You back!" Believe me, friend, things are going to happen on earth between now and then that will make us desperately anxious to see Him back. God is going to arrange that.

That is the primary purpose of God—the establishment of His Kingdom on earth visibly with a visible King ruling over it. Everything that God does is directed toward that. Until we make that our priority, we are not really aligned with the will and purpose of God. That is why Jesus told us to pray for God's Kingdom to come. We are required to align ourselves with His purpose.

Prayer is not a way for us to get God to do what we want. A lot of Christians think it is. It may work out that way, but that is not its purpose. Prayer is a way for us to become instruments for God to do what He wants. When we become aligned with God's purpose, we are going to pray prayers that are irresistible. There will be no power, human or satanic, that will be able to resist the outworking of our prayer.

Your Will Be Done

Then Jesus said this in His prayer: "Your will be done on earth as it is in heaven."

This does not mean everything is perfect on earth, but it means that in any given situation God's purpose and solution can be perfectly worked out. Do you believe that? You see, you will pray differently if you convince yourself that is true.

But remember this: If you say to God, "Your will be done," you are saying, "Not my will." I want to tell you this: God's will is best. Most of us have let the devil make us afraid of God's will. "If I embrace the will of God it means suffering. It means denial. I'm going to have to give things up." It could happen that way, but look at Revelation 4:11: "You created all things, and by Your will they exist and were created." I have pondered that verse many times, and I have come to realize that there could not be anything better than God's will. God's will is the best way for anything to be at any time. We should never be afraid of embracing it. And we do so without knowing what it will involve.

When Ruth and I were preparing for speaking engagements one time we were, theoretically, resting in Hawaii. Actually we were battling the forces of Satan. We came to a point where both of us were on the floor and said, "Lord, we embrace Your will without any reservation whatever. Whatever You will, we embrace it."

I think God was squeezing us, putting pressure on us, to bring us to that place of total surrender to His will. There is actually relief when you do that. You do not know exactly what you are praying for, but you know that you have a Father who loves you, who is omnipotent, who always wants the best for you.

As I look back over the years that I have walked with the Lord, again and again I thank God for the times when He did not let me have my way. I can see situation after situation where, if I had done things the way I wanted, the outcome would have been disastrous. And there are other times that He has led me to pray the kind of prayers that change nations, change situations, change families. I can say to the glory of God that I can see several points where history was changed by my prayers and the prayers of believers gathered together. It can be changed by your prayers, too. Let me give you two examples.

About a year after I was called into the British Army and had that dramatic personal encounter with the Lord, my unit was sent out to North Africa, and I found myself serving there as a hospital attendant. In the course of that experience I was granted the rather doubtful privilege of taking part in the longest retreat in the history of the British Army—more than seven hundred miles of continuous retreating—from a place named Alagalah in Libya to the very gates of Cairo. Let me say, to retreat for seven hundred miles is a wearisome and demoralizing experience, especially in a desert.

At that point the fate of the Middle East hung in the balance. If the Axis forces could press through and capture Cairo, they would command the Suez Canal, cut one of the main lifelines of the British Empire and, ultimately, the land of Israel, and the oil resources of the entire Middle East would be at their mercy.

Now, doubtless there were many factors that caused that retreat, but the one that impressed me was that the officers did not have the confidence of the men under them. The British officers were selfish, irresponsible and undisciplined. I am the son of army officers and I say this having considered exactly what I mean to say. One example was this. We lived on short quantities of water. A single bottle of water was all that a soldier was allowed for two days for all his needs—washing, shaving, drinking, cooking. And yet it was easy to see when you went into the officers' mess that they had more water on their tables to drink with their whiskey in an evening than the enlisted man had for every purpose for two days.

There I was, newly converted. I had not had any opportunity to attend church. All I had was the Bible and the Holy Spirit. I thought to myself, *I ought to be able to pray about this situation intelligently.* I knew I did not know what to pray. So I said in my naïve way, "Lord, show me how You want me to pray."

The Lord gave me a specific answer, which was this prayer: "Lord, give us leaders such that it will be to Your glory to give us victory through them." I was less than a year old in the Lord when I prayed that prayer. I prayed it consistently.

Now I did not know what was happening, but God began to move swiftly. The British government appointed a new commander for their forces in the Middle East in North Africa. This man was flown back to Cairo to take command but his plane crashed on landing and he was killed. So at that very important time in the most active theater of the war, the British Forces were left without a commander.

In that situation, Winston Churchill, who was prime minister of Britain at the time, acted more or less on his own initiative and appointed an unknown officer who was flown out from Britain. His name was Bernard Montgomery. Montgomery was a committed Christian and a God-fearing man. He was also a very fine commander and a man of great discipline.

He went to work reorganizing the British forces. He restored discipline and morale; he changed the whole attitude and bearing and conduct of the officers. And then there was fought the well-known battle of El Alamein, which was the first major Allied victory in the whole of that theater of war. It reversed the course of war in North Africa in favor of the Allies.

I was serving with a military ambulance up in the desert, a little way behind the advancing British forces. On the tailboard of the truck there was a little portable radio. I listened as a news commentator described the preparations at Montgomery's headquarters just before the Battle of El Alamein was fought. He described how Montgomery came out and assembled his officers and men and said this: "Let us ask the Lord, mighty in battle, to give us the victory."

As I listened to those words, what I call "heaven's electricity" went through me from the crown of my head to the soles of my feet. God spoke quietly but firmly to my spirit and said, *That is the answer to your prayer.*

Thus, I learned early in my Christian experience that prayer can change the course of history. I read an article in a British newspaper on the 100th anniversary of Montgomery's birth in which it said that no British general in human history has ever conducted a more brilliant campaign than Montgomery conducted at that time in North Africa. As I prayed, God raised up a man who would give Him the glory. Do you believe that? Can you believe that your prayers can change history? That God will do things for you as you pray?

Now, some people may say, "Well, that's arrogant. I'm sure there were other people praying." There certainly were other Christians in Britain praying. But this is true as well: Even if just one person prayed, and prayed the prayer of faith, and met God's conditions, God has committed Himself to answer.

There are only two alternatives about prayer. Either God answers prayer or He does not. If He does not answer prayer it is foolish to pray, and if He does answer prayer it is foolish not to pray. I believe He answers prayer. That is my firm conviction. But the lesson I want to emphasize here is God has got to give you the prayer. Receiving it is like taking hold of a spear. When you take it, hold it out. Keep it held out. Don't draw it back.

The second example of history-changing prayer I want to give you happened when I was working with students and teachers in Kenya in 1960. At that time Kenya was scheduled to receive independence from the British Empire within just a couple of years. The country had gone through a tremendous political crisis. The Mau-Mau emergency, which had torn the country in two, created enmity and suspicion, not only between blacks and whites, but also among the different African tribes. Just at that time the Belgian Congo to the west had received independence from Belgium and had immediately been plunged into bitter civil war. All the political experts predicted that Kenya would go the same way as the Belgian Congo, only worse.

In August of that year, I was one of the speakers at a Bible convention for African young people. The convention lasted a week and we had come to the closing night. The Spirit of God had come in a rather sovereign and unique way. At a certain point I felt that we had tapped the resources of God's Almightiness, and that it was our responsibility to use them aright. So I went up to the platform and silenced the young people who were praying. I then challenged them to pray for their nation's future. I pointed out to them that Christians have a responsibility to pray for their government and that their country was facing a major crisis. I told them that probably their prayers were the only thing that could save their country from disaster.

Those three hundred young people united in prayer for about ten minutes. They were praying, laying hold of God—it was one of the most dramatic experiences I have ever participated in. Then, when they became silent, the young African man who had been standing beside me on the platform spoke quietly to his fellow Africans.

He said, "I want to tell you that while we were praying I had a vision. I saw a man on a red horse—and the horse was fierce and cruel—was coming toward Kenya from the east. Behind it were other red horses, also fierce and cruel. But," he said, "while we were praying I saw those red horses turn around and move away from Kenya toward the north."

Then he said, "As I was meditating on this, God spoke to me and said this: *Only the supernatural power of the prayer of My people can turn away the troubles that are coming upon Kenya.*"

Now I cannot go in detail into the history of the years that followed, but I have to say that that vision granted to that young African was exactly fulfilled. About three or four years later a serious Communist attempt to move into Kenya from the east and take over the country was foiled by the wise and the prompt action of Jomo Kenyatta, the first president of Kenya. The Communists never made any real advance in Kenya. They moved away to the north and occupied Somalia, which became basically an armed Communist camp.

But from that time onward until now, Kenya has been one of the most stable and progressive of more than fifty new African nations that have emerged on the continent since World War II. Certainly that was not what the political experts predicted. It was brought about by prayer—by concerted, corporate, believing prayer at a time of crisis in the nation's destiny.

To be able to pray like that is worth more than all the fortune in this world. A person who can pray like that is more influential than the general who wins the victory or the government that controls the general.

I have not always prayed that God's will be done on earth as it is in heaven. Sometimes I am bogged down in my own petty concerns and my limitations and I begin praying about me, me, me. There is nothing wrong in asking God to help you, but it will not really produce the divine result until your whole attitude and motivation are aligned with God's purposes being done in the earth.

God is not going to change. If God and I are out of harmony, guess who is going to change? And besides, living out of harmony with God, especially if you are a Spirit-baptized believer, is painful.

How can we be in harmony? The answer is to align with God's purposes. The first keys to knowing His will are there at the beginning of the Lord's Prayer. "Our Father in heaven. . . ."

Knowing God's Will

One of my favorite passages, Romans 12, gives us further keys to discovering God's will. As I understand it, they are all here in the first eight verses.

> I beseech you therefore, brethren, by the mercies of God, that you present your bodies a living sacrifice, holy, acceptable to God, which is your reasonable service. And do not be conformed to this world, but be transformed by the renewing of your mind, that you may prove what is that good and acceptable and perfect will of God. For I say, through the grace given to me, to everyone who is among you, not to think of himself more highly than he ought to think, but to think soberly, as God has dealt to each one a measure of faith. For as we have many members in one body, but all the members do not have the same function, so we, being many, are one body in Christ, and individually members of one another. Having then gifts differing according to the grace that is given to us, let us use them: if prophecy, let us prophesy in proportion to our faith; or ministry, let us use it in our ministering; he who teaches, in teaching; he who exhorts, in exhortation; he

who gives, with liberality; he who leads, with diligence; he who shows mercy, with cheerfulness.

Verses 1–8

Paul began with *therefore* in verse 1. I always say that when you find a *therefore* in the Bible, you want to find out what it is there for. This *therefore* relates to the previous eleven chapters of Romans in which Paul outlined the whole message of God's mercy and grace. Then he asked, "In the light of that, what should we do; how shall we respond?" And the answer he gave was this: "Present your body a living sacrifice, holy, acceptable to God."

That always blesses me. The Bible is so down-to-earth. A lot of us would expect something super-spiritual. After all this glorious unfolding of the grace of God, we ask, "God, what do You want?"

And He says, "I want your body." You see, when He gets the body, He gets the contents.

Paul also says how we are to give it to Him: "Present your body to Him a living sacrifice." Why a living sacrifice? Because Paul was contrasting it with the Old Testament sacrifices, which were first killed and placed on the altar. Thus, Paul was saying, "Don't kill your body and place it on the altar. Place a living body on the altar."

When a sacrifice was placed on the altar it no longer belonged to the person who offered it; it belonged to God. It is as though God says here, "Place your body on My altar as a living sacrifice. From now on you don't own it. I own it. You don't make the decisions as to what will happen to your body—I make them. You don't decide where you are going to go; you don't decide what you are going to eat; you don't decide what you are going to wear. Those are My decisions. I take full responsibility for your body."

Give this careful consideration. Be careful when you make this commitment that you mean what you say. But also realize the benefits of such a dedication. God has a different attitude toward the property that is merely leased to Him as opposed to the property that is His. He accepts maintenance responsibility for what He owns. You might actually find that this is the answer to your problem. Give God your body. You have struggled with it long enough.

The next verse says: "Do not be conformed to this world [this age], but be transformed by the renewing of your mind, that you may prove what is that good and acceptable and perfect will of God."

In order to discover God's will, you have to have a change in your thinking. Your mind has to be renewed. God can do that, but He will not do it until He has your body. After you present your body, then He will renew your mind. And when your mind is renewed, you can discover the will of God. Lots of people get saved and I suppose they get to heaven at the end, but they never discover God's will in this life because their minds are never renewed.

Then Paul said in the next verse: "I say, through the grace given to me, to everyone who is among you, not to think of himself more highly than he ought to think, but to think soberly, as God has dealt to each one a measure of faith."

The renewed mind is not proud. It is not arrogant. It is not self-asserting. It is humble, sober, realistic. Suppose you get a job at a bank. The first day you walk into the bank to start work you do not expect to sit in the manager's chair. Just so, when you come into the Kingdom, you should not expect to be an apostle on day one. Be willing to be an office boy, to empty the wastepaper baskets. In the spiritual life, the way up is down. The lower down you start, the higher up you end.

And then Paul said, in effect, we are not going to make it on our own. We are going to have to be part of the Body of Christ. God has given us a measure of faith, a proportion of faith, suitable to our places in the Body. When we find our places, we will discover that we have the faith we need for those places and for those functions.

You see, my hand works wonderfully well as a hand, but if I try to walk on my hands I get into trouble. My hand is designed to be a hand and not a foot. Lots of Christians are feet trying to be hands or noses trying to be ears. If you have a continual struggle for faith in your Christian walk, it is almost guaranteed that you are trying to be something God did not design you to be. Basically the life of faith has tests and problems, but it flows. It is not a continual struggle. When you find your place in the Body, then your allotted proportion of faith that God has given you will make you successful in that place.

Then finally Paul said in closing this little simple outline, that when you are in your place in the Body, God will give you the gifts you need for that place. A lot of people are just interested in spiritual gifts—and I agree, they are exciting. But they are not to be sought in detachment from the Body. In fact, until you know your place in the Body you do not know what gifts you will need. My experience has been that when I get in the right place I have the right gifts.

I remember when God thrust me into the ministry of deliverance—helping people to be free from demons. A certain friend of mine brought his sister, a married woman, for deliverance, to Lydia and me in a hotel somewhere in Colorado. The woman sat there—and she was a picture of misery. She obviously had problems. I looked at her, opened my mouth and heard myself say, "You need to be delivered from . . ." and I named about eight demons. Instantly I thought to myself, *How did I know that?*

And then I realized that God had given me the gift of a word of knowledge. Why? As an ornament? No, because I needed it to be effective in the place where He had put me.

Do you see the importance of presenting your body a living sacrifice to God if you want to know His will for your life? I want to challenge you. Have you ever really handed over the control of your body to the Lord Jesus Christ? Have you said, "God, it's Yours. It's at Your disposal. Do with it what You want"? If you have not, there is no better time than now to make that decision.

This is a very serious decision—one that you do not want to make and then go back on. God does not expect you to be perfect from this moment onward, but He does expect you to be sincere and wholehearted. If you really have decided that this is the time that you are going to put your body on God's altar, I suggest that you pray this simple prayer:

Lord Jesus Christ, I thank You that on the cross You died in my place to save me from my sin and to make me a child of God. In response to Your mercy, Lord, I now present my body to You. I lay it upon the altar of Your service as a living sacrifice. From this time onward it belongs to You, Lord, and not to me. I thank You for receiving this sacrifice. In Jesus' name, Amen.

We are coming into days when we are going to see God's Spirit move on the earth more and more. Our commitment will be tried and tested as never before by the enemy who realizes that his time is short. In later chapters we will learn more about building up the Body into a house of prayer. First, however, we come to the topic of spiritual warfare and the weapons that we will need to pray effectively. Let's go on farther now in understanding God's will, moving into this deeper place of prayer.

6

SPIRITUAL WEAPONS
FOR SPIRITUAL WARFARE

I know a man in Christ who fourteen years ago—whether
in the body I do not know, or whether out of the body I do
not know, God knows—such a one was caught up to the
third heaven.

2 Corinthians 12:2

This verse brings us face-to-face with the revelation
that there is more than one heaven. Paul says he knew
a man—and, incidentally, I never have believed this
man was Paul—who had a marvelous experience of being
caught up into the third heaven where he "heard inexpress-
ible words, which it is not lawful for a man to utter" (2 Corinthians 12:4).

I believe we can assume that if there is a third heaven, there
must be a first and a second heaven. I want to look for a moment

at the placement and inhabitants of each of these heavens. This is important if we are going to pray victoriously.

In these verses Paul indicated that the third heaven is the location of Paradise. This is now the place where the departed spirits of the righteous go, but this was not always the case. There was a time when the abode of the righteous dead was down in Sheol, a special compartment of the lower part of the earth. You will remember that under the Old Covenant, Abraham and all the saints went down into a special place that was separated from the spirits of the departed wicked by a great gulf. After the death and resurrection of Jesus Christ, Paradise was translated. From that time on, Paradise has been up in the third heaven in the presence of Almighty God.

The Bible also speaks about something we could call the mid-heaven or second heaven. This word is taken from the book of Revelation. John said, for instance, "I saw another angel flying in the midst of heaven" (Revelation 14:6). That is actually one single compound noun that could well be translated "the mid-heaven." This second heaven is Satan's headquarters. From that position he and his angels do everything they can to bring destruction on earth and to resist the purposes of God's grace, blessing and mercy. More on that in a moment.

The first heaven is what we see when we go out at night and look up into the stars—the visible heaven. We might say that it is the roof of man's dwelling place.

So, we see that: God resides in the third heaven, and man resides near the first heaven. In between the two, in the mid-heaven, resides a rebellious kingdom of Satan and his fallen angels.

Now what does this have to do with praying prayers that God hears and answers? Quite a bit. It gives us a picture of spiritual conflict—the opposition we face when we pray.

The View of the Heavenlies

To understand spiritual warfare, we need to understand what we are fighting against. Scripture reveals that at the present time Satan's headquarters are in the heavenlies. Paul gives us a clear picture of this in his letter to the Ephesians: "For we wrestle not against flesh and blood, but against principalities, against powers, against the rulers of the darkness of this world, against spiritual wickedness in high places" (Ephesians 6:12, KJV). The King James Version, while quite familiar, does not give us the most accurate translation. Let's break this verse down into a more literal understanding of the Greek.

For we wrestle not against flesh and blood, but against principalities, against powers . . .

In Ephesians and other passages, the words *principalities* and *powers* are often joined closely together. The word *principality* is derived directly from the Greek word for *ruler*. The word *power* is the word for *authority*. So I prefer to say that our wrestling match as believers is not against flesh and blood, not against human beings, but against rulerships and the realms of their authority. It is also:

against the rulers of the darkness of this world . . .

A more literal wording of this would be: "Against the world rulers of the present darkness." The darkness of this present age has a world headquarters, from which it is ruled. The headquarters is the mid-heaven and the ruler is Satan. In Ephesians 2:2, Satan is called "the prince of the power of the air." He is, then, the ruler of the realm of authority that is defined by the air. Many people picture Satan living down in the bowels of the earth. He is not there; he is in the heavenlies.

Obviously he is not in the heaven that is God's dwelling; he was cast down from that. But neither is he on earth. Revelation 12:9 tells us that a time is coming when he will be cast down out of the heavenlies onto earth. Then it says he is going to make all the trouble he can in the short time that is left to him. (We will look at this in more depth in chapter 7.) But in the meanwhile, up to the fulfillment of that passage in Revelation 12, his headquarters are in the mid-heaven. We also wrestle:

against spiritual wickedness in high places.

The King James wording *high places* here is completely misleading. The same Greek word is used numerous times in Ephesians, and in each of these places it is correctly translated "heavenly."

Now let's view our more literal translation of Ephesians 6:12:

Our wrestling match is not against flesh and blood, but against rulerships and the realms of their authority, against the world rulers of the present darkness, against the spiritual forces of wickedness in the heavenlies.

This is our spiritual conflict. In the book of Daniel the Bible gives us a vivid picture of this battle in progress. Let's turn there.

The Battle in the Heavenlies

Daniel, taken from Israel to Babylon as a youth, remained a fervent student of the literature of his people. As such, he was aware that the prophetic timeline of the Babylonian captivity was coming to a close. "In the first year of his reign, I, Daniel, understood by the books the number of the years specified by the word of the LORD through Jeremiah the prophet, that He would accomplish seventy years in the desolations of Jerusalem" (Daniel 9:2).

Daniel began to pray for this approaching eventuality with a time of fasting. "In those days I, Daniel, was mourning three full weeks. I ate no pleasant food, no meat or wine came into my mouth, nor did I anoint myself at all, till three whole weeks were fulfilled" (Daniel 10:2–3).

Daniel saw what God had committed Himself to do and responded with this attitude: "God, I'm in this with You. Count me in. I'll give myself to prayer and fasting as I never have done before until I see the fulfillment of Your promise in experience."

We will explore in chapter 8 the theme of fasting as a powerful component of our prayers, particularly as regards the Church in the Last Days. For now we note that fasting is a kind of spiritual mourning. God has said that He will give the oil of joy to those who mourn in Zion (see Isaiah 61:3)—not the natural mourning of the flesh but the spiritual mourning of those who are concerned about the desolation of God's house and God's people.

Jesus said in the Sermon on the Mount, "Blessed are those who mourn, for they shall be comforted" (Matthew 5:4). Let me note that we must be very sensitive to the Holy Spirit about this. We should not try to mourn when the Holy Spirit is comforting us, and we should not try to work up excitement and a thrill when the Holy Spirit is calling us to mourning.

Daniel spent 21 days mourning, praying and waiting upon God. He did not fast completely, but he abstained from all except the most basic forms of food and drink. At the end of three weeks, the archangel Gabriel was sent to Daniel with a revelation of God's purpose for Israel in the Last Days. The rest of chapter 10 and the next two chapters of Daniel describe the advent of the angel, his appearance and the revelation that he brought. For our purposes of understanding spiritual warfare, let's look at the timeline of the angel's appearing. "Then he said to me, 'Do not fear, Daniel, for from the first day that you set your heart to understand, and to humble yourself before your God, your words were heard; and I have come because of your words'" (Daniel 10:12).

Daniel's prayer was heard the first day that he started to pray. But the angel did not arrive till three weeks later. What happened in the meanwhile? The next verse tells us. "But the prince of the kingdom of Persia withstood me twenty-one days; and behold, Michael, one of the chief princes, came to help me, for I had been left alone there with the kings of Persia" (verse 13).

When the archangel Gabriel spoke about "the prince of the kingdom of Persia," he was not talking about a human being. He was talking about one of the dark angels in the mid-heaven. Gabriel started on his journey the first day that Daniel started to pray; angelic warfare in the heavenlies withheld his arrival. The good holy angels were opposed and resisted by Satan's angels, the angels of darkness. But notice: It was Daniel's prayers on earth that got the archangel through. Do you see how important our prayers are? The archangel depended on Daniel and his prayer to get through.

Notice also that the initiative is with earth, not heaven. Daniel started the whole thing moving. And I venture to say, in certain respects this remains true today. We are not waiting for God; God is waiting for us. When we move, heaven will move. Then will come the conflict, and our prayers on earth will settle it. We who are believers and know how to pray are much more important than most of us have the faintest idea.

This Scripture shows us something else as well. It shows why we can pray for something in the will of God and not receive the answer immediately.

Picture it like this. The three heavens are on three different levels, one above the other. When the prayer of the believer goes up from earth, the angel bearing the answer comes down at God's word, leaving the third heaven. But in between the two, a wicked prince in the mid-heaven works to block the answer. When the believer "prays through" that conflict, the answer comes. The meeting point of the prayer and the answer is the breakthrough. That is why Jesus said, "Men always ought to pray and not lose heart [or give up]" (Luke 18:1). We often have to "pray through" in order to have the breakthrough that God intends for us. (We will learn more about this in chapter 8 on fasting.)

But notice the distinction. We are not "praying through" because of a hesitancy or reluctance on God's part, as some suppose. No, we are praying through satanic opposition in a kingdom in the mid-heaven set in direct opposition to all the good that God wants to do for us.

If you are sensitive to the Spirit, you will know when the breakthrough has taken place. There have been times in spiritual experience when I have known it is settled. Now we have the victory. Now we can dance. Now we can sing. The battle is finished. All that is left is to gather the spoils. We will see an illustration of this in a moment from the story of Jehoshaphat.

This is the basic picture of spiritual conflict as it is unfolded in Scripture. When the angel left Daniel he gave this further insight: "And now I must return to fight with the prince of Persia; and when I have gone forth, indeed the prince of Greece will come" (Daniel 10:20).

The prince of Persia was a satanic angel that dominated the kingdom of Persia. This was of particular importance to

Daniel because Persia was ruling over God's people, Israel. When the Persian Empire was defeated, the empire of Greece followed. Behind the empire of Greece was another satanic angel called the prince of Greece. This shows us that earth's empires have their counterpart in Satan's empire. In other words, Satan seeks to control the empires of earth through its rulers in order to make its leaders and governments instruments of his will. We must pray for our governments in order to frustrate Satan and to bring our governments under heaven's control.

That is why Paul said first of all—before you pray for the sick, the missionaries, the evangelists, even your family—to pray for the government. As we have seen, anyone who criticizes the government is telling the world that he has failed in his prayers. He has not done his job. He has allowed these dark angels to crowd in over the buildings where vital decisions are made that affect not only us but also the whole Kingdom of God. We must not tolerate that invasion of Satan.

Our Position in the Heavenly Places

The decisive factor in this great war with Satan is just one thing: praying believers. We are the ones who tip the scale for victory on God's side. This is an astonishing fact, but Scripture makes it clear that this is so. Our prayers are not unimportant; they are not secondary. They are the decisive issue in the entire spiritual conflict.

The way we pray will decide the way the universe goes.

I do not believe that is an exaggeration; I believe it is the literal truth. Nothing grieves me more than to hear believers talk as if they were unimportant. "It doesn't much matter what I say or what I do. I am basically insignificant." True, you are insignificant. That is the point. It is just because you are insignificant that God has chosen you for the demonstration of His wisdom, His grace and His power to the whole universe.

But this means that you are no longer insignificant. You are extremely significant! The whole universe revolves around you. I believe this. Paul said in 2 Corinthians 4:15: "All things are for your sakes." Everything is for our sake because of our relationship to Jesus Christ and because of what God is determined to do through us for the whole universe.

Paul helps us understand our position in the spiritual conflict. "Blessed be the God and Father of our Lord Jesus Christ, who has blessed us with every spiritual blessing in the heavenly places in Christ" (Ephesians 1:3). "[God raised Christ] from the dead and seated Him at His right hand in the heavenly places, far above all principality and power [all rulership and realm of authority]" (Ephesians 1:20–21). "[God has] raised us up together, and made us sit together [with Christ] in the heavenly places in Christ Jesus" (Ephesians 2:6).

Jesus has been exalted far above the realm that is Satan's headquarters. Further, we accept by faith that, in the Spirit, you and I are seated with Christ in the realm that is far above Satan and his realm. Physically we are down here on earth, but spiritually, because of our relationship with Christ, we are with Him: "To the intent that now the manifold wisdom of God might be made known by the church to the principalities and powers in the heavenly places" (Ephesians 3:10).

What a marvelous statement! The Church—we who believe in Jesus Christ—are God's demonstration of His many-sided wisdom to the whole theater of the universe.

You see, earth is not the center of the universe, but it is the stage. The writer of Hebrews says we are surrounded by so great a cloud of witnesses (see Hebrews 12:1). We are being watched from the third heaven by those who are cheering for us, and we are being watched from the second heaven by those who are booing against us. We are a spectacle, Paul says, to men, to angels, to the whole world, the whole universe. And God is showing in us—the weak, the unworthy, the base, the rejected—all the riches of His grace, His glory and His wisdom.

You know why God chose us? Because there is nothing in us that could ever take the credit. All the glory has to go to God. "The base things of the world and the things which are despised God has chosen, and the things which are not, to bring to nothing the things that are" (1 Corinthians 1:28).

Our Spiritual Weapons

If we are involved in spiritual warfare against a spiritual enemy, it is obvious that we must have spiritual weapons. Carnal weapons are of no use whatever for spiritual warfare. You cannot blast demons and rebellious angels out of the way with a tank.

This is what Paul said: "For though we walk in the flesh [though we live in the body], we do not war according to the flesh. For the weapons of our warfare are not carnal [not material] but mighty in God for pulling down strongholds" (2 Corinthians 10:3–4).

Whose strongholds? Satan's. Where does he have his strongholds? Maybe in the very head offices of your government at this time. Maybe there are men and women in vital administrative offices that are Satan's strongholds. Whose business is it to pull them down? Ours. And we have been given the weapons. The weapons of our warfare "[cast] down arguments and every high thing that exalts itself against the knowledge of God" (verse 5).

The great high thing that exalts itself against the knowledge of God is Satan's kingdom in the heavenlies. We have been given the weapons to cast Satan's kingdom down—and we are the ones who are going to do it. The weapons have been placed in our hands rather than in the hands of the angels, though the angels doubtless have their weapons.

God has provided us three main spiritual weapons: the Word of God, the name of Jesus and the blood of Jesus. We launch these weapons by these means: prayer, praise, preaching and testimony. Let's look at these briefly. (Further study on the blood of Jesus will be the topic of our next chapter.)

The Word of God

In Ephesians 6:14–17 Paul lists the spiritual armor that the Christian soldier needs for spiritual conflict. The first five items of armor are all defensive: girding our waist with truth, putting on the breastplate of righteousness, seeing that our feet are shod with the preparation of the Gospel of peace, taking up the shield of faith and the helmet of salvation. These protect the believer. There is no weapon of offense, or attack, until we come to the sixth item, which is the sword of the Spirit, which is the Word of God.

Here is the great weapon of attack. If you do not use the Word of God, you may be able to protect yourself, but you have nothing to attack Satan with. If you want to put Satan to flight, if you want to get him out of your way, out of your home, out of your family, out of your business, if you do not want just to tolerate him and hold him off, the weapon you must use is the weapon of attack—the sword of the Spirit, which is the Word of God.

The Word of God is translated here as the *rhema*, which usually denotes a word that is spoken. In other words, the

Bible lying on a bookshelf or nightstand is not an effective weapon. It is as we take Scripture in our mouths and proclaim it boldly that it becomes a sharp two-edged sword. Note, too, that it is the sword of the Holy Spirit. We can take God's Word in our mouths, but it only achieves its full effect when it is the Holy Spirit within us who actually wields it.

The perfect pattern of how to use the sword of the Spirit is provided by Jesus' encounter with Satan at the time of His temptation in the wilderness. Three times Satan approached Jesus with a temptation, and each time Jesus drove him back with the same phrase: *It is written* (see Matthew 4). Jesus used no other weapon but the *rhema*, the spoken word of the Lord.

God has made the same weapon available to each Christian. It is important, however, to bear two things in mind. First, Jesus had already been filled with the Holy Spirit (see Luke 4:1). It was the Holy Spirit in Jesus who directed Him in the use of the sword. And second, Jesus—like every Jewish boy of His day—had memorized long passages of Scripture. When Satan confronted Him, He did not need to consult a concordance or go to a library. He had already stored up the Scriptures in His memory. Surely we today need to do that just as much as Jesus did!

The Name of Jesus

Another powerful weapon for us to use is the name of Jesus. These two verses in Psalm 8 give us a unique understanding.

O LORD, our Lord, how excellent is Your name in all the earth, who have set Your glory above the heavens! Out of the mouth of babes and nursing infants You have ordained strength, because of Your enemies, that You may silence the enemy and the avenger.

Psalm 8:1–2

The enemy and the avenger is Satan, and God has given us the means to silence him. What good news! What is the weapon? It is the name of the Lord: "O LORD, our Lord, how excellent is Your name in all the earth." The channel that launches the name is the human mouth: "Out of the mouth of babes and nursing infants."

Spiritual things find expression out of the mouth. This is true for both good and evil. Look at Revelation 16:13, for instance. John saw three unclean spirits like frogs come out of the mouth of the dragon, out of the mouth of the beast and out of the mouth of the false prophet.

Why does the psalmist refer to the mouth of babes and nursing infants? To show that we do not have to be spiritual giants. God has chosen the weak, the foolish, the things that are despised to bring to naught all Satan's kingdom in the heavenlies.

In the gospel of Matthew we read that Jesus quoted this verse, Psalm 8:2, and gave us the interpretation. The Pharisees and the Temple rulers had come to Jesus complaining that there was too much noise in the Temple. People were dancing, clapping their hands, singing hosannas, and it upset the religious leaders. So they said to Jesus, "Don't You hear the noise? Is this the right thing to be doing in the Temple? Can't You call these people to order?"

Jesus gave them this response: "Have you never read, 'Out of the mouth of babes and nursing infants You have perfected praise'?" (Matthew 21:16). David wrote the words *ordained strength*. Jesus interpreted them as *perfected praise*. What does that tell us? That the ordained strength of God's people is perfect praise. When you praise the name of the Lord perfectly, you shut the devil up.

Can you see, my friend, why the devil is so busy trying to keep you from praising the Lord? When you effectively, perfectly, with your whole heart, in unison, with one accord praise the name of Jesus, it shuts the devil's mouth. And if ever there was a thing he does not like, it is to have his mouth shut. He will do everything he can—religious pressure, social pressure, fear of man—to keep you from turning loose in your prayers and praising the name of Jesus.

God has given me a kind of revelation like an inner TV screen on which from time to time I see all over the earth groups of believers gathered, all standing with one accord, their arms in the air praising and exalting the name of the Lord. God has shown me that when this happens the spiritual powers of darkness over that city or over that nation are broken. This is the way to drive out the infiltration of Satan's angels and demons. The air above our cities, our churches and our homes can be purified by perfect praise.

The Blood of Jesus

There is much I want to say about the blood of Jesus in relation to prayer; this will be the topic of our next chapter. But I want to make just one point here. Revelation 12:11 tells us: "They overcame him by the blood of the Lamb and by the word of their testimony."

Who is *they*? The believers on earth. Who is *him*? Satan. What I want to emphasize is that the final victory comes not to God's angels but to the believers. This passage describes war in heaven. Michael and his angels are fighting; Satan and his angels are fighting. But the believers overcame him by the blood of the Lamb and by the word of their testimony.

By testifying continually about the blood of Jesus they dislodged Satan from the heavenlies. Is that not a tremendous revelation? Can you see, my good friend, why the devil will do everything he can to shut your mouth? Except when you gossip about your neighbors! But when you want to praise Jesus or utter the Word of God or testify to what the Lord has done for you, Satan will put a barrier in front of your lips. Why? Because you are casting down his stronghold.

We have another example of a spiritual battle in the Old Testament story of Jehoshaphat. In this battle God's people gained total victory; their enemy was completely defeated. All they had to do was collect the spoils. I want to look briefly at the strategy of Jehoshaphat, the weapons that he used and how he gained this victory. I believe that every one of these principles and every one of these weapons applies exactly to us today.

Spiritual Victory

Jehoshaphat was king of Judah. He had just brought the people back to God and reestablished the Mosaic system of the Temple, the Law, the priesthood and the judges. He had done a wonderful job.

Then he was threatened by an invasion of a large host made up of Moabites, Ammonites, Edomites and others approaching his kingdom from the east, the direction of the Dead Sea. Jehoshaphat realized that he and his people were so outnumbered and the enemy had such superiority of numbers and military power that they could not meet them merely on the natural plane. So Jehoshaphat and the children of Judah moved the battle out of the natural realm and into the spiritual realm.

First, God's people fasted: "Jehoshaphat feared, and set himself to seek the LORD, and proclaimed a fast throughout all Judah" (2 Chronicles 20:3).

God's people were confronted with a life-or-death issue. They stopped "playing church" and set themselves to seek

141

the Lord. This was not a private individual fast; it was a collective fast of all of God's people confronted with immediate danger of military defeat and possible extermination. They knew the last great resort of God's people is collective fasting.

Second, they gathered together: "Judah gathered together to ask help from the LORD; and from all the cities of Judah they came to seek the LORD" (verse 4). In every major crisis in the history of Israel, God's people forgot their differences and came together.

The next thing was prayer:

> Then Jehoshaphat stood in the assembly of Judah and Jerusalem, in the house of the LORD, before the new court, and said: "O LORD God of our fathers, are You not God in heaven, and do You not rule over all the kingdoms of the nations, and in Your hand is there not power and might, so that no one is able to withstand You? Are You not our God, who drove out the inhabitants of this land before Your people Israel, and gave it to the descendants of Abraham Your friend forever?"
>
> 2 Chronicles 20:5–7

Notice that Jehoshaphat did not pray randomly. He prayed on the basis of the written Word of God as he knew it. He quoted God's Word back to Him.

This is a good example of praying God's will, of repeating to God what He has committed Himself to do. Jehoshaphat prayed exactly that kind of prayer. He took God back to the history of His people, the Old Testament records, the Law of Moses, the judges, the prophets. Jehoshaphat said, "God, You promised thus and so. Now do it. Do as You have said."

Next, as soon as he had finished praying, a prophecy came forth.

> Then the Spirit of the LORD came upon Jahaziel the son of Zechariah, the son of Benaiah, the son of Jeiel, the son of Mattaniah, a Levite of the sons of Asaph, in the midst of the assembly. And he said, "Listen, all you of Judah and you inhabitants of Jerusalem, and you, King Jehoshaphat!"
>
> Verses 14–15

Wherever God's people fast and come together in praise, there always will be prophetic revelation. I believe that prophetic ministry comes out of the fellowship of God's people earnestly seeking Him. No religious games, no parlor tricks, no spiritual cocktail parties, just desperate hearts before God.

This man came forth with prophecy and a word of wisdom. He said, "Don't be afraid. The battle is not yours; it is God's. You will not need to fight. All you have to do is go down tomorrow to a certain place called the ascent of Ziz, and you will find that God has dealt with your enemies."

Then they incorporated one more weapon: praise. "Then the Levites of the children of the Kohathites and of the children of the Korahites stood up to praise the LORD God of Israel with voices loud and high" (verse 19). The praises continued the next day:

> When [Jehoshaphat] had consulted with the people, he appointed those who should sing to the LORD, and who should praise the beauty of holiness, as they went out before the army and were saying: "Praise the LORD, for His mercy endures forever."
>
> Verse 21

The forefront of this army was a group of priests praising and singing. I would believe they were doing a little dancing, too. If I know anything about the Jews, they could not go on praising and singing without starting to dance. "Now when they began to sing and to praise, the LORD set ambushes against [their enemies]" (verse 22).

In the midst of their praises, the Lord dealt with the enemy. Oh, what a revelation! You minister to the Lord; He ministers to your problems. If God's people could only see this! Our weapons are mighty through God. We reach up to God and we split that mid-heaven of darkness between us. God reaches down and touches whatever problems we face as nations and individuals. When we use the spiritual weapons that God has given us, God will be just as faithful to us today as He was to Jehoshaphat and the children of Judah.

Every enemy coming against them in battle was destroyed. It took three days to gather the spoil! They came back to Jerusalem with Jehoshaphat in front praising the Lord, and the fear of God fell on all the kingdoms round about. They had no more problems with military invasions from then on (see verses 25–30).

Do you believe that can happen today? Do you believe that believers can do this around the world? May the Lord give us just a little spiritual glimpse of His greatness and His glory. And may we pray till all the hosts of heaven are bound, restrained and ultimately cast down.

7

GOD'S ATOMIC WEAPON:
THE BLOOD OF JESUS

And war broke out in heaven: Michael and his angels fought
with the dragon; and the dragon and his angels fought, but
they did not prevail, nor was a place found for them in heaven
any longer. So the great dragon was cast out, that serpent
of old, called the Devil and Satan, who deceives the whole
world; he was cast to the earth, and his angels were cast out
with him.

Revelation 12:7–9

The book of Revelation describes a war in heaven. Michael and his angels fought against the devil and his angels. The devil—that serpent of old—did not prevail. He was cast down out of heaven to the earth, and his angels with him.

Now I am aware that there are various ways of interpreting the book of Revelation. Personally I am convinced that the events described here in this passage are still in the future. I have studied interpretations of Revelation from what is called the historicist's school, which seeks to show that the events of history from the Christian era until now have been set forth in types and symbols and patterns and so on, but I am unable to believe it. As far as I am concerned, they do not do justice to the facts of history, and they do not do justice to the facts of Revelation.

Remember that the word *Satan* means literally "the resister." That is his name because that is his nature. Satan resists—deliberately and persistently—every purpose of God's grace, mercy and blessing. And he resists not merely God Himself but the people of God. The moment we profess faith in Jesus Christ, we are plunged into warfare. This revelation of future events, then, has great bearing on knowing how we pray now as Kingdom priests seeking to discern God's will.

I said, and it bears repeating, that the earth is not the center of the universe, but it is the stage of the universe. The apostle Paul said we are made a theater to the universe, to God, to men and to angels. At the present time the unseen realms are all gazing down upon us.

And on this little stage of this humble planet, the last great drama of the present age is being enacted. One event that helps bring the drama to a close is the casting of Satan and his angels out of the heavenlies onto earth. In other words, Ephesians 6:12 is still true. We are involved in a wrestling match with satanic forces—the spiritual forces of wickedness, lawlessness and rebellion who are in the heavenlies. Let's look at what is leading up to this final scenario a little more closely so that we can understand our current place of prayer.

Satan's Current Occupation

Revelation 12 gives us a glimpse at the current work of our enemy, which every one of us needs to remember: "The accuser of our brethren, who accused them before our God day and night, has been cast down" (verse 10). Satan at the present time has one supreme task, which he is very busy with. It is accusing you and me—*brethren* refers to believers—before the throne of God day and night. He finds every fault, every weakness, every flaw, every inconsistency that he can in our character, motives and conduct and reports it to God.

The Scriptures indicate clearly that before Satan fell he was a high-ranking angel. His commonly ascribed scriptural name *Lucifer* means "light bearer." At that time, when he was still in right relationship with God, his business was to bring reports from this area of the universe. When he fell and became a rebel, like a lot of other rebels I know, he tried to carry on as if nothing had happened. So he just goes on bringing his reports—extremely uncharitable, critical, bitter, cynical reports. He tears us to shreds with his descriptions of our motives and conduct.

And for the record, he does not need our help. We must not become critics of God's children, because the devil is doing all right without us. Above all, never become a critic of yourself. If you resort to self-condemnation, you are doing the devil's job for him in your own life. If you are a new creature in Christ, when you criticize yourself you are criticizing God's handiwork. That is not your job. Don't do it!

Our Answer in Jesus

The whole issue of our battle against evil centers in one thing: righteousness. Because of Jesus' righteousness, God has made it possible that the devil will have nothing to bring against us in heaven. "[God] made [Jesus] who knew no sin to be sin for us, that we might become the righteousness of God in Him" (2 Corinthians 5:21).

You can proffer the best Baptist lifestyle you have, the best Methodist principles, the best Roman Catholic piety, and he can tear it to shreds. But when you bring in the righteousness of Jesus Christ, he is silent. He has nothing more to say.

You will find that you can almost measure your spiritual progress by the extent to which you accept and appropriate by faith the righteousness of Jesus Christ on your own behalf. This is the great lesson that we have to learn as children of God. We are accepted in the Beloved not for what we are but for what Jesus is. The words of Jesus in Matthew 6:33 are often misunderstood: "Seek first the kingdom of God and His righteousness." In other words, not your own righteousness. In Romans 10:3 Paul wrote that the Jewish nation was attempting to establish its own righteousness. They had not submitted themselves to the righteousness of God by faith in Jesus Christ.

It takes humility to accept Jesus' righteousness because it means, first of all, we have renounced every shred of our old self-righteousness. "All our righteousnesses are like filthy rags" (Isaiah 64:6). Notice: Not our sins, but our righteousnesses are nothing more than filthy rags in the sight of God. As long as we flaunt the filthy rags of our church membership, our good deeds, our godly living, the devil will tear us to shreds in the presence of God. But when we come to the place where we are relying on nothing but the blood of Jesus Christ and His righteousness, there is nothing in us that the devil can put his finger on and bring up by way of accusation before God.

How Satan Is Overcome

At some point Satan will be cast out of heaven. Heaven will be purged.

"Therefore rejoice, O heavens, and you who dwell in them! Woe to the inhabitants of the earth and the sea! For the devil has come down to you, having great wrath, because he knows that he has a short time." Now when the dragon saw that he had been cast to the earth, he persecuted the woman who gave birth to the male Child.

Revelation 12:12–13

Rejoice, heaven—but look out, earth!

When the devil is cast down to the earth, he comes here knowing that he has only a few short years left. To me, it is clear that we are discussing a specific period of time, and the devil, who is a student of prophecy, knows it pretty well. When he comes down here, he knows he has "a time and times and half a time" (Revelation 12:14). This is generally accepted to mean three and a half years. Jesus said that those days will be cut short (see Matthew 24:22), so there will be at least a few days taken off at the end. Then the devil will be bound and imprisoned in the bottomless pit.

Now with this as background we learn more about our mission in prayer to procure the final defeat in casting down Satan.

Then I heard a loud voice saying in heaven, "Now salvation, and strength, and the kingdom of our God, and the power of His Christ have come, for the accuser of our brethren, who accused them before our God day and night, has been cast down. And they overcame him by the blood of the Lamb and

149

by the word of their testimony, and they did not love their lives to the death."

Revelation 12:10–11

The angels have their part to play, as they did with Daniel, but ultimately it is the believers on earth who eventually cast Satan from his place in the heavenlies.

Revelation 12:11 tells us not only that the believers will overcome Satan but also how they will do it. Look at this verse again, where the actual scene is described: "[The believers on earth] overcame [Satan] by the blood of the Lamb and by the word of their testimony, and they did not love their lives to the death."

These are people totally committed to God. Whether they live or die is not important to them. What *is* important is that they should fulfill their God-appointed function to overthrow Satan and cast him down. They do this using God's "atomic weapon": the blood of the Lamb and the word of their testimony.

You are probably aware of what is often referred to as "pleading the blood." I believe that the majority of Christians have never considered carefully and scripturally what it really means to use the blood of the Lamb by the word of our testimony. It is this: *Testify personally to what the Word of God says that the blood of Jesus does for you.*

The key words are *testimony*, *Word* and *blood*. You *testify* personally to what the *Word*, that is Scripture, says that the *blood* of Christ does for you. To make it effective you must make it personal. To whom are you testifying? To Satan. This is not a believer's testimony meeting! This is where you and I come face-to-face with the enemy of our souls. We speak directly to him in the name and the authority of the Lord Jesus Christ, and we tell him what the Word of God says that the blood of Jesus does for us.

About the Blood

In the next section we will view the statements made in God's Word about the blood. It is obvious that in order to be able to apply the Word of God we must know what it says. In fact, as long as anyone remains ignorant of the Word of God, ultimately, he or she will become prey to the devil. As we have seen, Scripture says it is your responsibility and mine to use "the sword of the Spirit, which is the word of God" (Ephesians 6:17).

Before we turn there I want to mention a remarkable Old Testament illustration of applying blood for deliverance. Exodus 12 is the Passover chapter. You will recall that the Passover was God's means to bring Israel out from the bondage, darkness and misery of slavery in Egypt. It is referred to throughout the Scriptures as the most vivid illustration of our deliverance from the bondage, darkness and misery of slavery to Satan and sin.

The whole of Israel's deliverance out of Egypt centered in the Passover lamb. On the tenth day of the first month, every household had to choose a lamb. On the fourteenth day at evening they had to slay those lambs. Ultimately, protection would come only through the blood of a lamb applied on the outside of the door of every Israelite's home in Egypt. God said that when He saw the blood on a doorway, He would "pass over" that house; the destroyer would not be allowed to come in.

When the lambs were slain, the blood was carefully captured, drop by drop, in a basin. Now the problem, if I may use that word, was to get the blood of the lamb to the doorway. The blood in the basin protected no one. If Israel had caught the blood in the basin and kept it there, not one Israelite home would have been protected. They had to transfer the blood from the basin to the doorposts.

God gave them one and only one authorized means to do that. He said to take a bunch of hyssop, a little herb that grows profusely and commonly all over the Middle East, and dip the hyssop in the blood. With the hyssop dripping with blood, they were to smite the lintel and the two doorposts of their homes. The hyssop, though it was a humble thing, was an essential part of the total plan of deliverance.

Notice also that the blood was to go on the lintel and on the two doorposts—not on the threshold. The blood is so sacred we must never walk over it. The book of Hebrews speaks about those who have trampled underfoot the blood of Jesus. The reference is to misusing the blood and applying it where it should not have been applied (see Hebrews 10:29).

This Old Testament story of application of blood is an analogy of our salvation in Christ. Paul wrote that "Christ, our Passover, was sacrificed for us" (1 Corinthians 5:7). He has been killed; His blood has been shed. In the terms of the analogy, the blood is now in the basin. But the blood in the basin does nothing for us. We have to transfer the blood from the basin to the place of our personal need—spiritual, physical, financial, family, business. Whatever our prayer may be, we have to get the blood of Jesus out of the basin and onto it. God has provided a means to do that.

It is not hyssop, of course. It is by our testimony that we transfer the blood from the basin to the door of our lives and personal needs. Christ has been slain; His blood has been shed. Protection is available. When I testify to what the Word of God says that the blood of Jesus does for me, that is like taking the hyssop, dipping it in the blood and sprinkling it all over myself. At that point I have the total protection and all the legal rights of the blood of Jesus over me, my situation, my body, my home, my life, whatever my prayer need may be.

By our application of the blood, the devil loses his opportunity to harass us, hurt us and invade our homes. He cannot pass through the blood.

The Word of Our Testimony

Now let's consider what the Word of God says that the blood of Jesus does for us. We will look at a number of statements in succession, and I will show you how to apply them in prayer with the hyssop of your personal testimony.

You might want to commit these verses to memory. If I stood upside down in a dark room on a dark night I could quote every one of these Scriptures without the least problem. I live by these Scriptures; I keep my hyssop in my hand. It is a rare day that passes without my using it.

Forgiven in Christ

Ephesians 1:7 tells us two things that we have when we are in Christ: "In [Christ] we have redemption through His blood, the forgiveness of sins, according to the riches of His grace."

Remember, when we are outside of Christ the blood does not avail. During the Passover in Egypt, the blood did not protect those who were not inside the houses. Here we see that inside Christ we have redemption and forgiveness of sins.

Redemption means "bought back by a ransom price that had to be paid." Let's look at another verse that tells us what we were redeemed from: "Let the redeemed of the LORD say so, whom He has redeemed from the hand of the enemy" (Psalm 107:2). This, by the way, is one of the most powerful Scriptures for teaching us the value of testimony. "Let the redeemed of the LORD say so" means to take the hyssop and use it.

Regarding our redemption, we were in the hand of the devil—did you know that? I have no problem knowing that I was in the hand of the devil, but I am not in the hand of the devil now because I have been redeemed out of it. But if I want the effectiveness of redemption through the blood of Jesus, I have to say so.

Here, then, is my testimony on the basis of Ephesians 1:7: *Through the blood of Jesus, I am redeemed out of the hand of the devil.*

This same Scripture tells me that all my sins are forgiven, so my next testimony is this: *Through the blood of Jesus, all my sins are forgiven.*

Meeting Conditions

Next is 1 John 1:7: "If we walk in the light as [Jesus] is in the light, we have fellowship with one another, and the blood of Jesus Christ [God's] Son cleanses us from all sin."

These verbs are all continuing present tenses indicating an ongoing process. If we walk in the light continuously, we will have fellowship continuously and the blood will cleanse us continuously. The cleansing by the blood of Jesus is not a single isolated experience; it is ever present.

If I am meeting the conditions—if I am walking in the light, if I am in fellowship with my fellow believers—then my testimony is this: *The blood of Jesus Christ, God's Son, continually cleanses me from all sin.*

Being Made Righteous

Romans 5:9 tells us that we are "justified by His [Jesus'] blood." The word *justified* is not understood by many present-day believers. *Just* and *righteous* are interchangeable terms both in Hebrew and in Greek, in the Old Testament and in the New. So *to be justified* means "to be made righteous."

What is it to be made righteous? This is my favorite definition: To be justified is to be just-as-if-I'd never sinned. When I am made righteous with the righteousness of Jesus Christ, it is as though I have never sinned.

Here is our next testimony: *Through the blood of Jesus, I am justified, made righteous, just-as-if-I'd never sinned.*

Being Set Apart

Hebrews 13:12 tells us that through the blood of Jesus we are sanctified: "That He [Jesus] might sanctify the people with His own blood, suffered outside the gate." The word *sanctify* is similar in form to the word *justify*. To *justify* means to "make just or righteous." To *sanctify* means to "make saintly or holy." The person who is made holy is set apart to God. In other words, when I am set apart to God I am not in the devil's territory. I am separated from the devil by the blood of Jesus.

God told Pharaoh in Egypt that He would make a redemptive difference between the people of Egypt and the people of Israel. The plagues that came upon Egypt would not come upon Israel, even though they dwelt there, because there was a redemptive difference. In our lives this difference is the blood of Jesus.

It was never the will of God for His judgment of the wicked to fall upon the righteous. If I am set apart to God by the blood of Jesus, then God's judgments on the wicked should never fall on me. I am not in the territory where those judgments apply.

Here is our next testimony. *Through the blood of Jesus, I am sanctified, made holy, set apart to God.*

Bought with a Price

The climax of our testimony is found in 1 Corinthians 6:19–20. I want to look first, however, at two other verses from this chapter in 1 Corinthians. Here is one: "Now the body is not for sexual immorality but for the Lord, and the Lord for the body" (verse 13). And then we read: "Do you not know that your bodies are members of Christ?" (verse 15).

Your body is for the Lord, and the Lord is for your body. If you do not misuse your body by uncleanness or immorality, by gluttony, drunkenness, nicotine or any of the horrible things that destroy the tissues and cells, if you set your body apart to the Lord, then you can say, "My body is for the Lord, and the Lord is for my body." But you must be sure that your body is for the Lord. And we have to include that unruly little member: the tongue.

Now we come to the climax:

> Or do you not know that your body is the temple of the Holy Spirit who is in you, whom you have from God, and you are not your own? For you were bought at a price [the price is the precious blood of Jesus]; therefore [because of the price that has been paid to buy you] glorify God in your body and in your spirit, which are God's.
>
> 1 Corinthians 6:19–20

The Lord wants you for Himself; He has paid the price of His precious blood. If you want to hold on to your own life you can, but remember, in that case, that you have not been bought. You cannot have it both ways. If you belong to God you do not belong to yourself. If you belong to yourself you do not belong to God.

When Jesus died on the cross, He paid the total price for a total redemption. He did not redeem part of you; He redeemed the whole of you. If you have accepted redemption through His blood then your spirit, your soul and your body are God's because Jesus paid the price of His blood to possess you.

This is our next testimony: *My body is a temple of the Holy Spirit, redeemed, cleansed, sanctified by the blood of Jesus. Therefore, Satan has no place in me, no power over me through the blood of Jesus.*

Now we can take all these Scriptures and unite them into a powerful testimony. And to quote a familiar phrase, buckle your seatbelt! In my experience this is the most powerful single way of dealing with Satan's power that I have ever experienced. If you make this confession in good faith, I would be very surprised if the enemy could endure it.

Actually, one of the great ministries of the Holy Spirit through the Word is to stir up the devil. Many people have said to me that they had a much more peaceful time before they were baptized in the Holy Spirit. That is not surprising because the Holy Spirit will force the enemy out into the open so that you can chase him out.

Here, then, is our testimony by which we apply the blood to our lives. The references precede each confession:

- *Ephesians 1:7*: Through the blood of Jesus, I am redeemed out of the hand of the devil.
- *Ephesians 1:7*: Through the blood of Jesus, all my sins are forgiven.
- *1 John 1:7*: The blood of Jesus Christ, God's Son, cleanses me continually from all sin.
- *Romans 5:9*: Through the blood of Jesus, I am justified, made righteous, just-as-if-I'd never sinned.
- *Hebrews 13:12*: Through the blood of Jesus, I am sanctified, made holy, set apart to God.

- *1 Corinthians 6:19–20*: My body is a temple of the Holy Spirit, redeemed, cleansed, sanctified by the blood of Jesus. Therefore, Satan has no place in me, no power over me, through the blood of Jesus.

If you really believe those words, the next thing to do is to praise the Lord for it. Here is a word of praise that you might use:

Thank You, God, for the precious blood of Jesus. Thank You for the redemptive blood of Christ. Thank You for the justifying, sanctifying, precious blood of the Lamb of God. Blessed be the name of the Lord. I praise You, Jesus, for You paid the price of my redemption. You shed Your precious blood on the cross. You are the Lamb slain from the foundation of the world. And now, Lord, I have taken the blood from the basin and transferred it to my own personal needs by the hyssop of my testimony. Amen.

Three Witnesses

Let me direct your attention to one more passage of Scripture that is relevant to this type of prayer. Speaking about Jesus, the Word says this:

This is He who came by water and blood—Jesus Christ; not only by water, but by water and blood. And it is the Spirit who bears witness, because the Spirit is truth. . . . There are three that bear witness on earth: the Spirit, the water, and the blood; and these three agree as one.

1 John 5:6, 8

This speaks about three witnesses. Two witnesses were all that were actually required for legal transactions in John's day. A third witness provides strong confirmation. The three witnesses are the water, the blood and the Holy Spirit.

Jesus came by water and blood. The water here is the cleansing of the Word. Jesus told His followers, "You are already clean because of the word which I have spoken to you" (John 15:3).

After the shedding of His blood, His further purpose became the sanctifying and cleansing of His Bride. Ephesians 5:25–27 says that Christ redeemed the Church by His blood that He might sanctify and cleanse her with the washing of water by the Word. He makes His Bride acceptable for Himself in this way.

The one who bears witness is the Holy Spirit. The Spirit bears witness because the Spirit is truth. So the Spirit, the water of the Word and the blood shed on the cross agree in one.

When we come to this place of divine agreement among these three witnesses in our lives, we have overcome Satan. The testimony that I have taught you is true; it uses the Word to testify to the blood. It is when the Spirit bears witness that the real effect comes.

In other words, there is nothing in the Christian life that is just a set of rules. Salvation is not a technique. Healing is not a technique. Deliverance from evil spirits is not a technique. Anybody who tries to reduce any of these things to a set of rules misses the point. The purpose of it all is this: When we use the water of the Word, when we use the blood in our testimony, and when the Spirit bears witness, then heaven's floor drops out and heaven comes to earth.

This is the place where we must come if we are going to have the prayer results that you and I need. Look once more at the testimony, without the references this time, and the prayer of command with which it closes. Let the Holy Spirit bear witness.

Through the blood of Jesus, I am redeemed out of the hand of the devil. Through the blood of Jesus, all my sins are forgiven. The blood of Jesus Christ, God's Son, cleanses me continually from all sin. Through the blood of Jesus, I am justified, made righteous, just-as-if-I'd never sinned. Through the blood of Jesus, I am sanctified, made holy, set apart to God. My body is a temple for the Holy Spirit, redeemed, cleansed, sanctified by the blood of Jesus. Therefore, Satan has no place in me, no power over me, through the blood of Jesus. I renounce him, loose myself from him and command him to leave me in the name of Jesus. Amen.

8

FASTING: OUR RESPONSE TO GOD'S PURPOSES

Consecrate a fast, call a sacred assembly; . . . and cry out to the LORD.

Joel 1:14

Throughout this book we have been learning that God wants to answer our prayers. As we ask within the will of God, meeting various conditions, our prayers will be answered. We also realize that the enemy is trying to hinder us; we have a responsibility to pray through until the answer comes.

Suppose, for instance, God has stated that it is His will to heal you. If He has given you the promise of healing, that is not the time to sit back and say, "I'm leaving it up to God. If it's His will, He is going to do it anyhow." That is as far from being in line with the mind of God as a person could possibly be.

The appropriate response is this: "God, You have promised. Thank You. I will seek You with all my heart for the fulfillment of what You have promised."

This is the prayer that God desires us to pray when He moves to fulfill the promises of His grace on behalf of His people. He wants us to seek Him even when He has told us what He plans to do. This is true not only for individual requests, but also for promises regarding nations and the world.

In this chapter we will look at a promise of God that affects believers particularly: What does God want to do for His people in these Last Days? And what is our response to be? Scripture answers both of these questions.

A Proper Response

Let's start with a prophetic Scripture about Israel that helps us understand further our proper response to God's stated purposes. This prophecy in Ezekiel concerns the national restoration of Israel, and it also applies to God's purposes for the Church. Actually, many things in the natural restoration of Israel—the fig tree—are patterns and examples for the spiritual restoration of the Church—the vine.

The latter part of Ezekiel 36 is a promise from God to restore the people of Israel to their own land and inheritance. Probably the greatest single objective proof that the Bible is an up-to-date and reliable book is the fact that God is restoring Israel to her own land. If there were never any restoration of Israel, we would have to take our Bibles and throw them away as worthless books because the entire Bible is committed to that fact.

Starting at verse 24 and going through verse 30, we find that God says more than a dozen times in those seven verses that He will do certain things for the house of Israel for the sake of His holy name (see verse 22). In other words, God's intervention is not due to Israel's merits; it is God's faithfulness to His promises and concern for the glory of His own name that moves Him to intervene in this way. Look at just the first two verses of this passage:

> For I will take you from among the heathen, and gather you out of all countries, and will bring you into your own land. Then will I sprinkle clean water upon you, and ye shall be clean: from all your filthiness, and from all your idols, will I cleanse you.
>
> Ezekiel 36:24–25, KJV

God says here certain things that He is going to do. Four times He says, "I will." And yet look at His words at the close of this great prophecy: "Thus says the Lord GOD: 'I will also let the house of Israel inquire of Me to do this for them'" (verse 37).

The Hebrew for the word *inquire* means "to seek God with great earnestness." Even though God has stated what He is going to do, He still desires that His people seek Him earnestly about it. I see in this verse a principle in God's relationship and dealings with His praying people: *God's predestined purpose provokes man's free response according to God's foreknowledge.*

He says, in effect, "When you see Me intervene on your behalf in this way, when you see My promises coming into fulfillment, I expect a response from you. Of your own free will, I expect you to turn to Me in humility and to seek me earnestly in prayer for the completion of what I have promised and what you have already seen begin to take place."

In other words, when God begins to move in sovereign grace on behalf of His people, fulfilling the prophecies and the revelations of His Word, and when God's people see these promises coming into fulfillment, then we do not sit back and say, "Isn't that wonderful! Look what God is doing!" That is not the appropriate response. The response should be: "God is moving on our behalf. Let us seek Him with all our hearts that He may fulfill the good word He has promised." As we learned in chapter 6, there will come a time to dance: when the battle is finished. That is the time to gather the spoils. But until then, knowing God's will should provoke us to a new measure of spiritual earnestness.

God's Purpose for His Church

Let us ask, then, an important question: What is God's purpose for us, the Body of Jesus Christ? What has God revealed that He will do? What do we see Him doing at this time?

Two Scriptures provide our answer. The first is Acts 2:17, which gives a sovereign declaration of what God will do for His people in the last days. It says this: "It shall come to pass in the last days, says God, that I will pour out of My Spirit on all flesh; your sons and your daughters shall prophesy, your young men shall see visions, your old men shall dream dreams."

Thank God He did not say, "I will pour out My Spirit if the churches unite" or "if the theologians concur" or "if the bishops permit" because it would never happen. God says, "No matter what happens, I am going to do this. This is My sovereign grace. This is My predestined intervention on behalf of My people. I will pour out My Spirit on all flesh. Your sons and your daughters will prophesy. Your young men will see visions. Your old men will dream dreams."

When Peter quoted that statement on the Day of Pentecost, he linked it directly with a prophecy from the book of Joel that addresses the restoration of God's people in the Last Days. I believe that if we look at Joel 2:25 we will find the key word that describes what God is doing in this outpouring of His Holy Spirit: "I will restore to you the years that the locust hath eaten, the cankerworm, and the caterpillar, and the palmerworm, my great army which I sent among you" (KJV).

The key word is *restore*—a national restoration of Israel and a spiritual restoration of the Church. God's purpose at this present time as revealed in Scripture is restoration of His people through the outpoured Spirit. Acts 2:17 says: "I will pour out of My Spirit." Joel 2:25 says: "I will restore."

We have seen this happening for decades all over the world. It is not because there are such wonderful preachers or such wonderful Bible teachers that we see these results. No human can take the credit for it. It is God's faithfulness to His Word that He will pour out His Spirit on all flesh. Every sector of the human race, without an exception, is going to experience this Last Days' outpouring of the Holy Spirit.

God said to Israel, "I will take you from the heathen, I will put you in your own land, I will sprinkle clean water upon you, I will cleanse you from all your sins and all your idols and your filthiness." God says concerning the Church, "I will pour out My Spirit upon every section of the Church. There will come a tremendous supernatural visitation."

We see this being fulfilled. The next question then becomes: What is our response to this great move of God?

Turning with All Our Hearts

Let's look again at the book of Joel. The outline of this short prophetic book is simple: desolation, restoration, judgment. Here is what God requires of His people in order to be delivered from desolation and to enter into restoration. The Lord says: "Consecrate a fast, call a sacred assembly; gather the elders and all the inhabitants of the land into the house of the LORD your God, and cry out to the LORD" (Joel 1:14).

Cry out to the Lord indicates desperate intercessory prayer. Gather the people of God into the house of God and then cry out to the Lord. Further, unite fasting with prayer. Not privately, but publicly, collectively.

Joel 2:12 says again: " 'Now, therefore,' says the LORD, 'turn to Me with all your heart, with fasting, with weeping, and with mourning.' " And then beginning in verse 15 we read:

> Blow the trumpet in Zion, consecrate [sanctify, set aside] a fast, call a sacred [solemn] assembly; gather the people, sanctify the congregation, assemble the elders, gather the children and nursing babes. . . . Let the priests, who minister to the LORD, weep between the porch and the altar.
>
> Verses 15–17

Blowing the trumpet indicates public proclamation. It is always a sign of warning and calling God's people together. While all are called, notice the particular emphasis upon the leaders—the elders, the ministers and the priests.

Here is one place today in the Church where anyone who is going to lead had better lead. A certain spiritual leader I know said to me, "Frankly, I have to run to keep up with the people I'm supposed to be leading." I want to challenge every leader, if you are a leader, you had better lead. And *lead* means "go ahead." Otherwise the eager laypeople will go ahead of their official leadership. When this call to fasting comes forth from the Word of God, the priests, the ministers and the leaders have an obligation to take the initiative and show real leadership.

Joel 2:28 speaks of the promise of restoration: "And it shall come to pass afterward, that I will pour out my spirit upon all flesh" (KJV). Now where Joel says *afterward*, Peter says *in the last days*. That is permissible because the Holy Spirit gave him that application. But I want to tell you that Peter's *in the last days* does not set aside Joel's *afterward*.

Afterward is another of those words, like *therefore*, that calls us to take a second look. Any time we consider the word *afterward* we have to ask, "After what?" The answer is: after we have done what God tells us to do. What did God tell us to do? Sanctify a fast. Call a solemn assembly. Turn to Him with all our hearts, with fasting and weeping and mourning. After that, God says that He will pour out His Spirit upon all flesh.

All that we have seen hitherto of the outpouring of God's Spirit is just a little sprinkle in relationship to what God has declared that He will do. We have seen Him move. We know that this is the hour. Now is it up to us to respond. It is up to us to move in and unite ourselves with what He is doing so that His purposes may come to complete fulfillment.

How do we move in? I want to suggest to you that God is calling His people with new emphasis to prayer and fasting. We have addressed the topic of fasting in several places in this book. We know that it means going without food deliberately for the sake of spiritual accomplishment. Fasting is a part of the total provision of God for His believing people. It is part of our spiritual discipline. Not only is fasting the revealed will of God for every professing Christian, but it is particularly the will of God for us at this time of the outpouring of God's Spirit.

Let's take a look now at the theme of fasting in connection with restoration.

Two Kinds of Fasts

Fasting has a particular relationship to the work of restoration. The great Old Testament chapter on fasting, Isaiah 58, sets forth two kinds of fasts—one that does not move the arm of God and one that does.

Verses 3–5 describe the fast that is not acceptable to God. The reason is that the attitudes and relationships of the people involved in it are wrong. They are resentful, they are grasping, they are covetous, they are legalistic, they are censorious, they are critical of others. God says that if we fast with that attitude and spirit, we cannot expect Him to hear us or to answer our prayer.

Verses 6–12 outline the kind of fast that He desires. As we look at each verse briefly, notice the number of promises associated with the kind of fasting that is acceptable to God.

I do not know any passage of the Bible that contains a more condensed list of tremendous promises than verse 6: "Is this not the fast that I have chosen: to loose the bonds of wickedness, to undo the heavy burdens, to let the oppressed go free, and that you break every yoke?"

Notice that the motive for fasting must be right. Regarding "letting the oppressed go free," I will tell you that in this ministry of deliverance there are people who will never be delivered until God's people—and primarily God's ministers—are willing to pay the price of prayer and fasting.

Then verse 7: "Is it not to share your bread with the hungry, and that you bring to your house the poor who are cast out; when you see the naked, that you cover him, and not hide yourself from your own flesh?"

Fasting must be accompanied by an attitude of genuine practical charity toward those who are in need. Some evangelicals are so evangelical that they have forgotten that the Gospel includes loving our neighbor as ourselves. This is a very practical form of love that God requires. God says that if our motives are right, if our attitudes and relationships are right, then He will tell us about the fast that He has chosen and what it will do for us.

Verse 8 says: "Then your light shall break forth like the morning, your healing shall spring forth speedily, and your righteousness shall go before you; the glory of the LORD shall be your rear guard [or shall gather you up]."

The promises in this verse are close to the promise of Malachi 4:2: "To you who fear My name the Sun of Righteousness shall arise with healing in His wings." This relates to the same period of time—these Last Days. To us who fear God's name, the Sun of Righteousness is now arising with healing in His wings.

The essence of the promise of Isaiah 58:8 is light, righteousness and healing. Jesus, the Sun of Righteousness, came to bring righteousness for the soul and healing for the body. God promises that when we begin to fast and seek Him in the right way and with the right motives, then will come light, righteousness and healing.

Continuing with verse 9: "Then you shall call, and the LORD will answer; you shall cry, and He will say, 'Here I am.' " God will be right at your elbow to answer your prayer, immediately at your disposal.

Then in the second half of verse 9, God warns again that wrong attitudes can spoil this. He says: "If you take away the yoke from your midst, the pointing of the finger, and speaking wickedness." We can sum those up in three phrases. The yoke is legalism. The pointing of the finger is criticism.

Speaking wickedness is insincerity. If we will give up legalism, criticism of others and insincerity, then God says He is ready to hear.

Verse 10 says: "If you extend your soul to the hungry and satisfy the afflicted soul, then your light shall dawn in the darkness, and your darkness shall be as the noonday." When we see the need for practical charity, light will take the place of darkness.

Verse 11 says: "The LORD will guide you continually, and satisfy your soul in drought, and strengthen your bones; you shall be like a watered garden, and like a spring of water, whose waters do not fail."

Whenever I read this verse, I want to know how I can get what it promises. Something in me says, "Lord, show me the way there." The way there is stated in verse 6. "Is not this the fast that I have chosen?" When we fast like this, we can expect guidance, direction and positive, clear assurance of God's presence and leading in every situation. No matter how dry it may be around you, you will have a fountain in your soul.

At times I have lived in areas of drought. It is easy to pick out the people who water their gardens and those who do not. The difference is tremendous. In the same way, the people who meet God's conditions, even when everybody else around them is dry and withered and parched, will be like a watered garden.

And then we come to the promise that culminates these promises of God. Verse 12 is the promise of restoration: "Those from among you shall build the old waste places." Did you know that there are a lot of old waste places in the church that need to be rebuilt? "You shall raise up the foundations of many generations."

I have made a brief study of individuals who really moved God and man in the history of the Church. They laid the foundation of many generations because their ministry extended beyond their own ages. If you consider the great modern evangelists—John Knox, John Calvin, Martin Luther, John Wesley, Charles Finney—every one of these individuals on his own testimony practiced fasting. If you want to lay the foundation of many generations, this is what goes with it.

Then we come to the last promise, verse 12: "And you shall be called the Repairer of the Breach, the Restorer of Streets to Dwell In."

There are many, many breaches in God's people's inheritance that need to be built up. We recall that God said in Ezekiel 22, "I sought for a man among them who would make a wall [or hedge], and stand in the gap before Me, . . . but I found no one" (verse 30). The prayer of intercessory fasting is making a wall (or a hedge, KJV) and standing in the gap. It makes us repairers of the breach.

There is a great pattern of restoration recorded in Old Testament history: It is the return of God's people from captivity in Babylon to their own land and the rebuilding of God's Temple in Jerusalem. We have viewed this in connection with the life of Daniel. Let's look at the lives of two men and one woman who were also associated with this great process. Chronologically, these were Ezra, Nehemiah and Esther. Each practiced fasting.

Ezra

When we turn to the book of Ezra, we go back in our Bibles but forward in time. Ezra was leading a party of returning exiles from Babylon to the city of Jerusalem. They came to the point where they were about to take a journey of several months through a country that was infested by brigands and hostile tribes. They had with them their wives, their children and—what was even more important to Orthodox Jews—all the sacred vessels of the Temple that had been captured and taken to Babylon.

One consequence about testifying to people is that you must live up to your testimony. This is one good reason for testifying. Ezra had made this bold testimony to the king of Persia: "Our God looks after His servants. God is equal to any situation, any danger, any emergency." Now that they were about to undertake this dangerous journey, He thought, *I can't go back to the king and say that we are fearful and ask for soldiers and horsemen to go with us. That would spoil my testimony. What are we going to do?*

Ezra was faced with the choice between two ways of doing things: the carnal and the spiritual. The carnal way would be to depend on the soldiers and horsemen, but he had shut himself off from that possibility. He was left with only one alternative: the spiritual. What form did the spiritual take? Prayer and fasting.

> Then I proclaimed a fast there at the river of Ahava, that we might humble ourselves before our God, to seek from Him the right way for us and our little ones and all our possessions [the gold vessels of the Temple]. For I was ashamed to request of the king an escort of soldiers and horsemen to help us against the enemy on the road, because we had spoken to the king, saying, "The hand of our God is upon all those for good who seek Him, but His power and His wrath are against all those who forsake Him." So we fasted and entreated our God for this, and He answered our prayer.
>
> Ezra 8:21–23

God heard their prayer. The power of prayer and fasting bound every robber, every brigand, every hostile tribesman, every kind of epidemic and disease that waited for them along the way. They came through in peace and in safety without losing a single member of their party and having preserved the beautiful Temple vessels.

This is one of the great lessons of the Bible. If you win the victory in the spiritual realm, you have won the victory, period. This is why the Bible is such a relevant book. Everybody is seeking answers to political, social and economic problems. If a nation by prayer and fasting wins the victory in the spiritual realm, all of the human realms will fall into line. Win the battle in the spiritual realm over Washington, D.C., for instance, and stand back and watch the economic, the political and the social problems fall into line.

Nehemiah

The next man in this process of restoration is Nehemiah, after whom the next book of the Bible is named. Nehemiah heard from some of his brethren: "And they said to me, 'The survivors who are left from the captivity in the province are there in great distress and reproach. The wall of Jerusalem is also broken down, and its gates are burned with fire' " (Nehemiah 1:3).

Nehemiah's response is found in the next verse: "So it was, when I heard these words, that I sat down and wept, and mourned for many days; I was fasting and praying before the God of heaven" (verse 4).

Nehemiah had learned the secret. The way was closed; the situation was hopeless. He fasted and prayed and God opened the way. God did not merely open the way for Nehemiah; He also obtained for him from the king full authority and provision to rebuild the city of Jerusalem. All this came through prayer and fasting.

Esther

Turn now to the fourth chapter of Esther. This is the greatest single crisis that has ever confronted the Jewish people in their entire history up to the present time—greater even than the crisis under Adolf Hitler. Hitler had only one-third of the Jews at his mercy; the Persian emperor had the entire Jewish nation.

Evil men under Haman, who was Satan's advocate against the Jews and the king's high official, had gained access to the king and obtained a decree by which all the Jews in the provinces of the kingdom of Persia would be exterminated on a certain day.

The book of Esther has given rise to the Jewish festival of Purim, which is the Hebrew word for *lots*. The festival has that name because Haman cast lots for a whole year to find the right day on which to exterminate the Jews. The fact that he cast lots indicates that he treated this as a spiritual matter; he was seeking supernatural direction. He also had wise men, or magicians, who advised him. This is the course that ungodly people often take when they realize that they need more than natural wisdom. They turn to the satanic supernatural for counsel.

This was a spiritual conflict between the forces of light and the forces of darkness, the power of the Holy Spirit and the power of Satan. Both had their agents and representatives right on the spot. The answer to the supernatural power of Satan invoked by Haman was the supernatural power of God invoked by Esther. When Esther heard the news, she said to her Uncle Mordecai, "Gather all the Jews who are present in Shushan, and fast for me; neither eat nor drink for three days, night or day. My maids and I will fast likewise. And so I will go to the king, which is against the law; and if I perish, I perish!" (Esther 4:16).

On the fourth day, Esther put on her royal apparel, went into the king's court and found favor in his eyes. He stretched out the golden scepter and said, "What do you wish, Queen Esther?"

The planned extermination of God's people was transformed into their greatest and most glorious success in the annals of the Persian Empire. Israel was saved and Haman was hanged on a gallows. What changed the whole situation militarily, politically? The prayer and fasting of Esther, her maidens and the Jews.

Four Principles of Fasting

The Word of God shows many basic principles related to fasting. Here are four: self-denial, self-humbling, right priorities and dependence upon God. Let's look at them briefly.

Self-Denial

Jesus said in Matthew 16:24: "If anyone desires to come after Me, let him deny himself." Fasting is denying your old rebellious ego. To deny, in one simple word, is to say no. Your stomach says, "I want," and you say to your stomach, "You don't dictate!"

Paul said in 1 Corinthians 9:27, "I discipline my body and bring it into subjection, lest, when I have preached to others, I myself should become disqualified."

He said that those who strive for mastery in athletic contests are temperate, self-controlled in all things (see verse 25). How much more should we be who are striving for mastery in the spiritual contest? A professional athlete is careful about what he eats, how much he sleeps. He even watches his mental attitudes because they affect his prospect of success. How much more do we as Christians have to be sure that we have brought our bodies under control!

A number of years ago God told me this: *If you want to go forward, there are two conditions. The first condition is that all progress is by faith. If you're not willing to go forward in faith, you cannot go forward. The second condition is this: If you are going to fulfill the ministry that I have for you, you will need a strong, healthy body. And you're putting on too much weight; you'd better see to that.*

That is exactly how God spoke to me. Believe me, in the years that have since elapsed, I have come to see that I do need a strong, healthy body. I do everything in my power to keep myself spiritually, mentally and physically fit, for the one thing that matters more to me than anything else is fulfilling God's calling on my life.

Self-Humbling

Fasting is self-humbling. We have talked about humility from the standpoint of 2 Chronicles 7:14: "If My people who are called by My name will humble themselves. . . ."

How do you humble yourself? David wrote about this in two of his psalms, Psalms 35:13 and 69:10. In each of them he said, "I humbled my soul with fasting." Some people pray, "God, make me humble," but that is not a scriptural prayer. God says, "Humble yourself." He can humiliate you, and He might have to. But the only person who can make you humble is you yourself. And one good way to humble your soul is with fasting.

Right Priorities

Fasting asserts right priorities. We looked earlier at Jesus' directive to "seek first the kingdom of God and His righteousness" (Matthew 6:33). Lots of people are seeking God's Kingdom second, third or fourth. The promises do not apply in that case. We have to have our priorities right. Fasting is a way of giving right priority to the spiritual, asserting its preeminence.

Dependence upon God

Fasting also demonstrates our dependence upon God. Fasting tells God, "God, I don't have the answer. I can't do it. I'm looking to You." It acknowledges dependence upon God, and it leads to divine intervention. Innumerable illustrations can be provided from Scripture to prove that when God's people meet His conditions along these lines, God answers with intervention on their behalf.

When, Not If

In the middle of the Sermon on the Mount, Jesus said, "When you fast" (Matthew 6:16).

Jesus did not say *if*. That would have left open the possibility that we might or might not fast. He said *when*. He took it for granted that we would fast. He used exactly the same language in this passage about three things: showing charity (verse 3), praying (verse 5) and fasting. In each case it is *when*, not *if*. Is it a Christian duty to show charity? Is it a Christian duty to pray? Then it must also be a Christian duty to fast.

Some people quote Jesus' words in Mark 2:18 as proof that we do not have to fast. In this passage, the people had come to Him and asked why the Pharisees fasted, the disciples of John fasted, but the disciples of Jesus did not fast. Jesus answered this way:

> Can the friends of the bridegroom fast while the bridegroom is with them? As long as they have the bridegroom with them they cannot fast. But the days will come when the bridegroom will be taken away from them, and then they will fast in those days.
>
> Mark 2:19–20

Here is how I understand this parable. The children of the Bridegroom are the disciples. The Bridegroom is the Lord Jesus Christ. While the Bridegroom was personally present on earth, His disciples did not fast. But Jesus said the time would come when the Bridegroom would be taken from them and in those days they would fast.

We ask ourselves this question: Is the Bridegroom now physically present with us or is He absent and we are waiting for His return? My answer is that we are waiting for His return. He has been taken from us and we will fast if we are His disciples. If we are not fasting, we lack one mark of discipleship.

The Pattern We Follow

Jesus practiced fasting (see Matthew 4:1–2). Five prophets and teachers in the church of Antioch fasted and waited upon God publicly and together (see Acts 13:1–2). God spoke to them and said to send out Barnabas and Saul (also known as Paul). They fasted and prayed the second time and sent them out (verse 3). Saul and Barnabas, on their first missionary journey, met with the converts that they had left behind and prayed with fasting (see Acts 14:23). Every one of those New Testament churches was brought into being by public prayer and fasting. Paul was often in fasting. It was one of the things by which he approved himself a minister of Christ (see 2 Corinthians 6:4–5; 11:27).

God has shown us the power of fasting if we want to see answers to our prayers—not least of which are our prayers for His Church in these Last Days. His grace and faithfulness provoke a response of our free will to turn to Him and to seek Him. Let us come with renewed earnestness and zeal, confidence and faith to see His purposes fulfilled.

9

THE GLORIOUS CHURCH

Christ also loved the church and gave Himself for her, that
He might sanctify and cleanse her with the washing of water
by the word.

Ephesians 5:25–26

We are a Kingdom of priests, and as such we are
called to pray. What is the ultimate goal of our
prayers? That the true Church will stand victorious, complete, ready for the return of Jesus. This is God's
directive for us in His Word—and the fulfillment of every
longing in our hearts.

Many people associated with the Church today have no
concept whatever of what it means to pray for or even speak of
the glorious Church. Yet Scripture says that the Church—the
Bride for which Jesus is coming—will be glorious. The Greek
word for *glory* is *doxo*, from which we get the English word
doxology, meaning "that which ascribes the glory to God."

I came to New Testament Greek by way of classical Greek,
the more ancient form of Greek. I have mentioned that I was

a student and a teacher of the philosophy of Plato, and one of the basic concepts of Plato's philosophy is summed up in this word *doxo*. There is a distinction about this word that used to puzzle me. In Plato's works, the word *doxo* did not signify "glory" but rather "that which seems to be, that which appears, opinion."

Being a bit of a revolutionary, I decided while I was studying philosophy that I would read the gospel of John in Greek during one of my summer vacations from Cambridge University. I announced to my tutor of Greek that I was going to do this, and he sought earnestly to dissuade me. He said it would spoil my classical Greek style. All I needed was to have my tutor try to dissuade me in order to make me determined to do it! So in the course of vacation, I read the gospel of John through in Greek.

Now I was far from God at this time. I made no profession of being a Christian. I was a professional philosopher, but somehow this message gripped me. I remember riding on a train from the west country, from Somerset. Back in London at Paddington Station, I was met by a fellow student and friend of mine. I said to him, "You know, I've solved the riddle of John's gospel." Just like that. I forget how I had solved it, but I had solved it!

What really gripped me in John's gospel, though, the thing that really puzzled me was this: John's use of the word *doxo* was translated in English as "glory." I remember wondering how that could be, since the more ancient classical Greek used the word in a different sense.

Some years later the Lord met me in that army barrack room in the middle of the night, and I was wonderfully born again of the Spirit of God. Less than two weeks later I was baptized in the Holy Spirit in the same room. At that time a flood of light came into me and many, many things that I had read earlier from the Bible came pouring back to me—as if I had read them just five minutes previously. Suddenly I understood this use of the word *doxo* that had so puzzled me.

In classical Greek it means "that which is seen, that which appears." In New Testament Greek it means "glory." This is because God's glory is that which appears. It is His visible, tangible presence made manifest to man's senses.

Stephen, speaking to the Jewish council, as recorded in Acts 7, said that "the God of glory appeared to our father Abraham when he was in Mesopotamia" (verse 2). I tell you that Abraham knew God by His glory. That was what marked Him out. He appeared in visible glory to Abraham when he dwelt in Mesopotamia. This so changed Abraham's life, motives and ambitions that he forsook all to go out into the Promised Land.

This brings us to the Church. When Scripture speaks about a glorious Church, it means a Church that is filled with God's glory, a Church that has within it the manifest, visible, tangible, personal presence of Almighty God. It is not a Church that is living on naked faith without any manifestation, but a Church that, through faith, has entered into a relationship with God where His visible, personal, tangible presence is with His people. The Bible says that is the kind of Church for which Jesus is coming. It is this Church for which we pray.

The Seven Marks of Christ's Church

We have been given in the epistle of Ephesians seven distinctive marks of the true Church of Jesus Christ as she will be in the day when the Lord comes for her. "Christ also loved the church and gave Himself for her, that He might sanctify and cleanse her with the washing of water by the word" (Ephesians 5:25–26).

We saw in chapter 7 that Jesus redeemed the Church by His blood that He might sanctify her by the pure water of His Word. The blood and the water of the Word are both needed to make the Church ready for the coming of the Lord.

I do not believe that any Christian will be ready to meet the Lord who has not gone through the sanctifying, cleansing process of being taught and disciplined by the Word of God. The blood of Jesus is the redemptive price by which we are bought back out of the hand of the devil. After we have been redeemed by the blood, we are then sanctified and cleansed by the washing of the water by the Word. Jesus' purpose in this is that He might present the Church to Himself as "a glorious church, not having spot or wrinkle or any such thing, but that she should be holy and without blemish" (verse 27).

The first three marks of the true Church, the Church for which Jesus will come, are stated there. She is to be (1) glorious—marked out by the manifest presence of God in her midst; (2) holy; and (3) without blemish.

If we turn back to Ephesians 4, we find the process by which this Church will be made ready for the coming of the Lord. Verse 11 speaks of the five main "body building" ministries of the Church: "He [Christ] Himself gave some to be apostles, some prophets, some evangelists, and some pastors [shepherds] and teachers." He gave these ministries "for the equipping [or perfecting] of the saints for the work of ministry" (verse 12).

The five basic ministries should equip the saints to do the work of the ministry for the edifying or building up of the Body of Christ. The next verse describes the goal: "Till we all come to the unity of the faith." The Greek says: "into the unity of the faith." It is the terminus toward which we are moving, along with coming into "the knowledge of the Son of God" (verse 13). The Greek word means not merely "knowledge" but "acknowledgment"—or the acknowledging of Jesus, the Son of God.

The way by which we will come into the unity of the faith is only through acknowledging Jesus Christ. It is not by sitting and discussing doctrine. If there is one sure thing, discussing doctrine does not unite Christians. The only way in which we will be united is by coming together around the headship of the Lord Jesus Christ. As we acknowledge Christ in His headship and in His supreme authority over every aspect of the Church, then we will come into the unity of the faith.

You see, the doctrine of salvation is meaningless without the Person of the Savior. The doctrine of healing is meaningless without the Healer. The doctrine of deliverance is meaningless without the Deliverer. The baptism in the Holy Spirit is meaningless without the Baptizer. When we acknowledge the Savior, we believe in salvation. When we acknowledge the Healer, we believe in healing. When we acknowledge the Deliverer, we believe in deliverance from evil spirits. When we acknowledge the Baptizer, we believe in the baptism in the Holy Spirit.

In every case, the road into unity is not the road of doctrinal disputation and discussion; it is the acknowledging of the Lord Jesus Christ in His glory, in His authority, in His headship and in every aspect of His ministry. As we acknowledge Christ in all that He is to the Church, we are brought into the unity of the faith.

Through this we are brought into two further parts of God's will. First: "to a perfect man" (verse 13). The word *perfect* would more plainly be translated "into a mature, full-grown man."

And then: "To the measure of the stature of the fullness of Christ" (verse 13). The key word there, I believe, is *fullness*. Until the Church of Jesus Christ, as His Body, demonstrates Christ in all His fullness—in every aspect, in every grace, in every gift, in every ministry—then the Church is not equipped to manifest Jesus.

You see, at the present time we manifest to the world a pathetically small part of the totality of Jesus Christ. There is much of Jesus that the Church is incapable of demonstrating to the world, but God is going to bring the corporate Body into that place where she will reveal the totality of Jesus Christ—in His personality and in His ministry. This is what is meant by fullness.

So we have altogether the seven distinctive marks of the Church as God is preparing to make her for Himself that He may then take her to Himself. She shall be (1) glorious—filled with the manifest presence of God; (2) holy; (3) without blemish; (4) coming into the unity of the faith; (5) acknowledging Jesus Christ in His headship and Lordship; and, thus, she (6) will come into maturity and (7) will manifest the fullness of Christ to the world.

In Ephesians we find a wonderful prayer of the apostle Paul for the Church:

> For this reason I bow my knees to the Father of our Lord Jesus Christ, from whom the whole family in heaven and earth is named, that He would grant you, according to the riches of His glory, to be strengthened with might through His Spirit in the inner man, that Christ may dwell in your hearts through faith; that you, being rooted and grounded in love, may be able to comprehend with all the saints what is the width and length and depth and height—to know the love of Christ which passes knowledge; that you may be filled with all the fullness of God.
>
> Ephesians 3:14–19

What I want to point out is that none of us can comprehend this individually. It is only as we come together with our fellow believers with all saints together that we are able to comprehend the totality of Jesus Christ—the height, the depth, the width and the length.

Paul prayed that the Church would "know the love of Christ which passes knowledge; that you may be filled with all the fullness of God" (verse 19). Is that not a most tremendous statement—that the Church of Jesus Christ is going to be the dwelling place of all the fullness of God? The totality of God in all His nature, in all His power, in all His aspects will be manifested in the Church.

There is only one other place that I know of in the Bible where the phrase *the fullness of God* is used, and that is in Colossians 2: "For in Him [Jesus] dwells all the fullness of the Godhead bodily" (verse 9). In Christ, God was manifested. Totally. Not partially, but totally. Notice from the Ephesians passage above that the Spirit is the one who ministers the glory and makes it available. When the Holy Spirit has completed the work of forming the Body of Christ, the fullness of God will again be manifested.

Do not ever imagine that this will happen to you on your own. It is only as you come together with other believers into the unity of the faith and the acknowledging of Christ that you will be able to comprehend with all saints the width and the length and the depth and the height of God, and thus be filled with all the fullness of God. This is the purpose of God for the Body of Christ, the Church.

How This Will Happen

The prophet Isaiah gives us an outline of how this will come to pass. Isaiah 59:19–60:5 gives us the picture. Let's take it verse by verse.

"So shall they fear the name of the LORD from the west, and His glory from the rising of the sun" (verse 19). God is going to manifest Himself in such a way that the whole earth will fear Him and will see His glory.

"When the enemy comes in like a flood, the Spirit of the LORD will lift up a standard against him" (verse 19). The truth is, the enemy has come in like a flood. We can see in the United States that the enemy, the devil, has infiltrated every area of national life in the past few decades—political, social, the schools, the colleges, the seminaries, the universities. Not only has he come in like a flood in the world, but, above all, he has come in the churches. Most of us do not need to be convinced of that.

This is the fulfillment of the prophecy of Joel where the people of God and their inheritance are desolated by an invading army of insects. The Church has been invaded through the centuries by God's great army of judgment. The cankerworm, the locust, the caterpillar, the palmerworm, they have all moved in and desolated the inheritance of God's people. But God says that His Spirit will move among us. When the enemy shall come in like a flood, then the Spirit of the Lord shall lift up a standard against him.

The standard that the Spirit of God uplifts is just one Person, and that is Jesus Christ. The Holy Spirit does not uplift a human personality; He does not exalt a doctrine; He does not exalt an institution. He has come to the Church to do one thing. Jesus said, "When He, the Spirit of truth, has come . . . He will glorify Me, for He will take of what is Mine and declare it to you" (John 16:13–14). The ministry of the Holy Spirit within the Church is to reveal, uplift, magnify and glorify the Lord Jesus Christ.

In ancient times, when an army was hard pressed and in danger of defeat, the standard bearer was instructed by the commander in chief to find a piece of elevated ground, stand there and lift up the standard. When the soldiers in that army, looking around, saw the uplifted standard, it was a sign to them that they were to gather and regroup around the base of the standard.

This is what has been happening in recent decades in the Church. As believers are praying, the Holy Spirit has begun to uplift the standard, Jesus Christ. From every section of the Church God's hard-pressed people, in danger of being overrun, scattered and finally defeated, have raised their voices in prayer, turned around and seen an uplifted standard. This is not a denomination, not a church, but the Lord Jesus Christ.

God is regathering His people. That is the subject of Isaiah 59:20: " 'The Redeemer will come to Zion, and to those who turn from transgression in Jacob,' says the LORD."

The people of God will return to the Lord, and the Lord will return to His people. We have to repent and turn from our backsliding, our carnality, our self-sufficiency, our sectarianism, our rebellion. When we turn from our transgressions to the Redeemer, we find that the Redeemer has come to Zion. Restoration has come to the people of God.

So God goes on to declare in this context:

"As for Me," says the LORD, "this is My covenant with them: My Spirit who is upon you, and My words which I have put in your mouth, shall not depart from your mouth, nor from the mouth of your descendants, nor from the mouth of your descendants' descendants," says the LORD, "from this time and forevermore."

Isaiah 59:21

This restoration is not partial nor is it temporary. It is final and it is permanent. This is the great final restoration of the Spirit of God to God's people who have been living so many centuries like orphans without the Comforter. This restoration is forever.

Dispelling the Darkness

In chapter 60—though there is a chapter division I believe the prophecy is consecutive—we notice a tremendous contrast between light and darkness. The message is for God's people, for Zion:

> Arise, shine; for your light has come! And the glory of the LORD is risen upon you. For behold, the darkness shall cover the earth, and deep darkness the people [of the earth]; but the LORD will arise over you, and His glory will be seen upon you.
>
> Isaiah 60:1–2

This is where we are just now. Darkness is covering the earth, and yet grosser darkness is going to cover the peoples of the earth. Let's be realistic. The Bible reveals it clearly and we can see many evidences of a kind of darkness that we have never even contemplated before beginning to engulf the inhabitants of the earth. But in the midst of the darkness the message of God to His people is that the glory of the Lord is risen upon us.

Here is the contrast. The light is getting brighter; the darkness is getting darker. We have come absolutely, conclusively to the parting of the ways. Neutrality from now on is ruled out. Jesus said that anyone who is not with Him is against Him (see Matthew 12:30).

Every one of us is going to have to make a decision and make a commitment. Do we love the light? We will come to the light. If we refuse to come to the light Jesus said it is because our deeds are evil. Light has come into the world and men love darkness rather than light (see John 3:19). This is the choice that confronts each one of us. Am I going to walk in the light? Am I going to be identified with the light and the purposes of light in the earth? Or am I going to hide away in the darkness as it grows darker and deeper across the face of the earth?

I would like to give you three Scriptures that I believe all illustrate the truth of this growing divide. The first is Genesis 15:5. Abraham was pleading with God about the sons that had been promised to him, for he had no sons. Scripture says the Lord took him out on a dark night and showed him the stars of heaven. "Count the stars," God said. "So shall your descendants be." Abraham believed God, and verse 6 tells us that God "accounted it to him for righteousness."

God showed me by revelation in the middle of a sermon once that this applies to us, for Galatians tells us that through faith in Jesus Christ we are the children of Abraham (see Galatians 3:7).

Normally speaking, we do not pay much attention to the stars. But when the sun has set, when the moon is not shining and when every natural source of light has been extinguished, it seems that the stars shine brighter than you ever saw them shine before. That is precisely how it is going to be at the close of the age. As darkness covers the earth and gross darkness the peoples, as the night gets darker and darker, the children of Abraham, through faith in Jesus Christ, are going to shine out like the stars in their glory. This is the place we are approaching.

The second Scripture is in the Song of Solomon. Here is a sudden glimpse of the Bride coming forth in her glory: "Who is she who looks forth as the morning, fair as the moon, clear

as the sun, awesome [terrible, KJV] as an army with banners?"
(Song of Solomon 6:10).

The world recoils in amazement. The world has never seen a
Church like this. Who is this coming forth like the morning? In a
night of darkness, she is as fair as the moon. The business of the
moon is to reflect the glory of the sun. And you know, of course,
that the moon appears in phases. It waxes and wanes.

The Church of Jesus Christ has waxed and waned. But when
she comes around to full moon, the world is going to see a full-
orbed Church, reflecting the glory and brightness of the Son.
She will have the authority of the Son of righteousness, Jesus
Christ, imputed to her. She will be as terrifying as an army with
banners. Who has seen a Church like this—terrible to the forces
of evil and darkness, sin and Satan? The Church is coming forth
that will cause the forces of Satan to tremble and flee.

One thing God has shown me about the devil is that there
is a message he fears more than any other message. It is the
message of what the Church is going to be and what the
Church is going to do to the devil. I believe that the devil
fights against this truth more than against any other.

The third Scripture that shows us the growing divide between light and darkness is in Revelation. This is the same
truth brought out in another way. The last book and almost
the last verses of the Bible say this:

And he [the angel] said to me [John], "Do not seal the words
of the prophecy of this book, for the time is at hand [the end
time]. He who is unjust [or unrighteous], let him be unjust
[or unrighteous] still; he who is filthy, let him be filthy still;
he who is righteous, let him be righteous still; he who is holy,
let him be holy still."

"And behold, I [Jesus] am coming quickly, and My reward
is with Me, to give to every one according to his work."

Revelation 22:10–12

You see, the time is at hand. Jesus is coming quickly. And what is the message? Listen: It is a fearful message. He that is unrighteous, let him be still more unrighteous. He that is filthy, let him be still more filthy. He that is righteous, let him be still more righteous. He that is holy, let him be still more holy. You cannot stand still; you will go up or down. To be stationary, to be static, to be neutral is no longer possible. If you want deliverance, I will tell you one thing: You had better get desperate. And do not expect the preacher to be desperate for you.

I remember a man who called me for counsel about a problem. His problem was pornography. He was a youth leader in a well-known, large church of a well-known denomination, but he was gripped with pornography. He said his room was filled with pornographic volumes, and he could not keep away from dirty movies.

I told him how to repent, how to be delivered. The next year I was in the same area again, and the same man phoned me for help with the same problem. I said, "You had your chance. Why didn't you act on what I told you last year?" He said he was ready to come and see me. I made an appointment; he did not keep it. He phoned me the next day and said, "I'm sorry I didn't keep that appointment; I went to a dirty movie."

Do you know what I said to him? I said, "You'd better go on and live it up because you don't have long." He that is filthy, let him be more filthy still because he has not got much longer. Those are the words of Scripture. I had never thought of that verse in that light but—oh!—how it applied to that man. A man involved in filth and yet pretending that he wanted deliverance.

If you are unrighteous, go on, friend, live it up. If you are filthy, get filthier still because you do not have long. And if you are righteous, do not trust in your righteousness. Be more righteous. If you are holy, be more holy. Nothing deceives God's people so much as to believe their salvation is a static condition that you arrive at by going forward at the altar of a church, saying a little prayer and shaking the pastor by the hand. That is a caricature of salvation. Salvation is not a static condition; it is a way of life.

Proverbs 4:18 says this: "The path of the just [the righteous] is like the shining sun, that shines ever brighter unto the perfect day." Job 17:9 says this: "The righteous will hold to his way, and he who has clean hands will be stronger and stronger."

Millions of churchgoing people are deceived about what salvation is. I have to acknowledge a certain measure of responsibility for allowing them to be deceived. I have preached a message of salvation that was not in line with the Word of God. Salvation is not a merit badge received for having sat fifteen years in a church pew. It is a way of life that is progressive. If we are not moving in the way of righteousness, if the light is not getting brighter on our pathway, we are going astray. The path of the righteous is as the shining light that shines more and more until the perfect day.

The Result of This Glory

What will be the result of the Church manifested in glory? I believe these next three verses of Isaiah 60 tell us: "The Gentiles shall come to your light, and kings to the brightness of your rising" (verse 3).

Nations and rulers will turn to the Church. Do you know that the majority of rulers of the nations today are at their wits' end? They do not have an answer to their problems, and they know it.

I believe that when the Church is what she should be, we will have the rulers of the nations lined up at our door asking for the answer in the dark hours that lie ahead. It is coming. In order to be ready, we must be fervent in prayer.

Daniel and Joseph were two such men who remained constant in prayer and affected the ruling of nations. In the critical hours of two great Gentile empires, the rulers went to these young Jewish men who had more than natural wisdom. They had an answer from God—and it placed them immediately in the highest positions of authority in those Gentile empires. The God of Daniel and the God of Joseph is the God of the Church of Jesus Christ. Like Daniel and Joseph, we need to be able to go to the Lord for an answer and take it to the rulers.

In Isaiah 60:4, we read that the young people come in. The Church is told this: "Lift up your eyes all around, and see: they all gather together, they come to you; your sons shall come from afar, and your daughters shall be nursed at your side."

There is a great deal in the Last Day prophecies about young people. Look at Acts 2:17: "It shall come to pass in the last days, says God, that I will pour out of My Spirit on all flesh; your sons and your daughters shall prophesy, your young men shall see visions, your old men shall dream dreams." There is a tremendous influx of young people coming into the Church of Jesus Christ. It has already started. In recent years we have witnessed baptismal services—for instance, on the West Coast of the United States—in which four and five thousand young people were immersed in the sea and testified of their faith in Jesus Christ.

I have it deeply laid upon my heart that we should have an answer for these young people when they come. I do not believe that they will ever get into the institutional church as we know it. And my prayer is: God forbid that they should! We have a responsibility to give them a simple pattern of Christian life and discipline that they can apply without becoming fossilized and institutionalized as you and I have been for so many years.

The fifth verse of Isaiah 60 tells us what will happen to the Church. This is the one I love. "Then you shall see. . . ." The Church is beginning to see after being blind for centuries who God is and what God is doing. And the next thing is that the Church will flow together (see verses 5–7). Lots and lots of little streams are trickling down from lots and lots of different areas, and they are all joining one great stream that is becoming a river. This river is going to become a great river. It is going to flow forth into a mighty ocean that shall fill the earth with the knowledge of God as the waters cover the sea.

The first time God ever gave me the gift of interpretation, I had been baptized with the Holy Spirit about 48 hours. I spoke in an unknown tongue, and without realizing it I began to interpret. I did not know what it was, but I knew that I was not choosing the words that I was saying. I was astonished. And I remember the words as clearly as if they happened last night: *It shall be like a little stream; the stream shall become a river; the river shall become a great river; the great river shall become a sea; and the sea shall become a mighty ocean.*

I believe it. At that point, if you had talked to me about revival I would not have known what you were talking about. I had no doctrinal knowledge of Scripture, no background in evangelical circles, nothing. This first time God ever spoke to me individually, He told me what He was going to do. These many decades later, I am at the point where I see the great river beginning to flow.

But that is not the end. The great river is going to become the sea, and the sea is going to become a mighty ocean. And here it is in the Word of God: "Then thou shalt see, and flow together" (Isaiah 60:5, KJV). Everyone who sees the uplifted standard of Jesus Christ is coming out from his little corner, his little hill place, his little valley, trickling down into one great stream.

When Ezekiel saw the living waters that flowed out of the Temple at the close of his prophetic book, they were initially just deep as the ankle. He went forward a thousand cubits and they were up to the knees. Another thousand cubits and they were up to the loins. In the next thousand they were waters to swim in, a river that could not be passed over. When the Church gets as deep as waters to swim in, she will not be passed over. The Church will no longer be irrelevant or out of date. When the river is flowing deep enough for us to swim in, the world will know we are here.

You know one thing I feel about the Rapture? It should be that when we are gone the world will miss us. At the present time I doubt whether the world would know the Rapture has taken place. But when we go, they are going to miss us. That is my conviction.

Verse 5 also says this: "The abundance of the sea shall be turned to you, the wealth of the Gentiles shall come to you." The wealth of the Gentile world is coming to the Church. God ordained three great structures to be built for His glory by His people. The first was the Tabernacle of Moses. The second was the Temple of Solomon. The third is the Church of Jesus Christ. I know there were other buildings, but none was in the same category as these three. Each one of these buildings had a divine pattern, each one had a divine provision and each one had a divine purpose.

Let's take a moment to look at the Temple of Solomon and I will show you what I mean. Then we will see the similarities to pray for within the Church.

Building the Temple

First Chronicles 28 gives the words of David in connection with preparation for the building of this great Temple. I want to give a significant portion of this Scripture to show the extent to which God directed the pattern.

> Then David gave his son Solomon the plans for the vestibule, its houses, its treasuries, its upper chambers, its inner chambers, and the place of the mercy seat; and the plans for all that he had by the Spirit.
>
> *Verses 11–12*

David got the pattern for the Temple by the Spirit of God, by divine revelation. Read further:

> Of the courts of the house of the Lord, of all the chambers all around, of the treasuries of the house of God, and of the treasuries for the dedicated things; also for the division of the priests and the Levites, for all the work of the service of the house of the Lord, and for all the articles of service in the house of the Lord. He gave gold by weight for things of gold, for all articles used in every kind of service; also silver for all articles of silver by weight, for all articles used in every kind of service; the weight for the lampstands of gold, and their lamps of gold, by weight for each lampstand and its lamps; for the lampstands of silver by weight, for the lampstand and its lamps, according to the use of each lampstand.
>
> *Verses 12–15*

Every item of gold and silver, the exact weight of gold and silver required to make that specific instrument, was provided specifically by David to the last dram.

And by weight he gave gold for the tables of the showbread, for each table, and silver for the tables of silver; also pure gold for the forks, the basins, the pitchers of pure gold, and the golden bowls—he gave gold by weight for every bowl; and for the silver bowls, silver by weight for every bowl; and refined gold by weight for the altar of incense, and for the construction of the chariot, that is, the gold cherubim that spread their wings and overshadowed the ark of the covenant of the LORD. "All this," said David, "the LORD made me understand in writing, by His hand upon me, all the works of these plans."

Verses 16–19

What a building when even the forks are made of pure gold! The entire pattern was given supernaturally by the Spirit of God. Every vessel, its exact structure, its pattern, its weight and the exact amount of gold or silver required to produce each vessel was all given by the Holy Spirit.

Once he had the pattern, David set out to procure the provision.

Furthermore, King David said to all the assembly, "My son Solomon, whom alone God has chosen, is young and inexperienced; and the work is great, because the temple is not for man but for the LORD God. Now for the house of my God I have prepared with all my might."

1 Chronicles 29:1–2

One reason God loved David so much was because he acted with all his might. When David did things, he did not do them by halves. He was wholehearted in worship, wholehearted in giving, wholehearted in consecration. He said:

Now for the house of my God I have prepared with all my might: gold for things to be made of gold, silver for things of silver, bronze for things of bronze, iron for things of iron, wood for things of wood, onyx stones, stones to be set, glistening stones of various colors, all kinds of precious stones, and marble slabs in abundance.

Verse 2

Does that make you feel wealthy? When I read that I begin to think what a wonderful God we have. There is no stinginess, no meanness, no narrow-mindedness with God. Everything about Him has to be abundant and glorious.

Then David gave from his own resources: "I have given to the house of my God, over and above all that I have prepared for the holy house, my own special treasure of gold and silver: three thousands talents of gold, of the gold of Ophir" (verses 3–4).

We can estimate that a talent of refined gold in the time of David would be worth minimally about $800,000 today. David out of his own fortune provided 3,000 talents of gold. That is about $2.4 billion. Did you ever stop to think of that? He started life as a little shepherd boy, but because of God's blessing, he could contribute billions of dollars worth of gold—and we won't even go into the calculation of the silver. That is the small change!

Then he challenged the people, who also offered willingly. They gathered 5,000 talents of gold (verse 7). More billions. And if you calculate the value of the other materials—the silver and the gems—plus all that had to be imported, like the cedars from Lebanon, plus the stones that were cut for the building, plus carvings and fabrics . . . the investment is almost incalculable.

Nothing was to be skimped. Nothing was to be second class. Everything was to be of the highest standard according to an exact pattern. And everything that was needed was provided to the last dram, item by item. For every gold candlestick, every gold fork, every gold plate, every gold dish, the exact amount of gold was provided and shaped according to the pattern. Why? Because of its purpose: It was for the glory of God.

"Body" Building

Now this is a picture of the Church of Jesus Christ. As we come to the close of this age, God is going to complete the greatest building that the world has ever seen. It is going to make the Temple of Solomon look insignificant. What building is this? It is the Body of Christ.

I believe in this generation it is God's purpose to complete this building. That means that just as the wealth of God's people was needed to complete the Temple of Solomon, so the wealth of God's people is going to be needed to complete the work of the Church of Jesus Christ on earth.

Now we have moved out of the spiritual and into the material. Or have we? What do you think? Do you believe it is unspiritual to talk about gold and silver? If so, then the Bible is a very unspiritual book, and the New Jerusalem is a very unspiritual place because its streets are paved with gold!

Listen, just as the Temple of Solomon required the wealth of God's people for its completion, so the Church of Jesus Christ is going to require the wealth of God's people for its completion. God is going to enable His people to give as abundantly to the Church as they gave to the Temple.

Do you know that this is one reason why I became an American citizen? You may laugh, but it is the truth. I am speaking in all earnestness when I tell you that I came to the conclusion as a Britisher relatively new to the United States that God had a special destiny and purpose for the United States of America. It is not easy for a Britisher to see that. We all know that God has blessed this nation materially, technologically, in every way as no nation has ever been blessed in the history of the earth.

I believe God has done this because He wants the wealth, the technology, the skills of the United States to be used to complete the house of God. I really believe that this is the destiny of God for the United States of America.

I pray toward that end. I have begun to claim the wealth of the United States for the Kingdom of God. There is nothing more tragic than to be blessed with material prosperity and have no vision as to how to use it. That is the tragedy of many in the young generation. Everything has been dumped into their laps, giving them abundance and no vision.

Now, friend, prosperity is a blessing. Poverty is a curse. Prosperity without vision is just frustration. What I want to give you is a vision. Are you willing to consecrate your service to the Lord? Are you willing to consecrate your prayers along with your earnings, your talents and your abilities to the Kingdom of God and the Church of Jesus Christ? That is the one thing that is going to stand when everything else crashes.

The Unshakable Kingdom

Turn with me to the prophet Haggai in closing. God has clearly forecast this in Scripture: "For thus says the LORD of hosts: 'Once more (it is a little while) I will shake heaven and earth, the sea and dry land; and I will shake all nations" (Haggai 2:6–7).

This is quoted in Hebrews 12 as the final great intervention of God in judgment on the nations. This is the final shak-

ing. God is going to shake everything that can be shaken—
insurance policies, cars, houses, investments in the bank can
all be shaken. What is going to stand is God's purpose: "And
they shall come to the Desire of All Nations" (Haggai 2:7).
This is the New King James Version, but the correct translation is "the treasures of all nations shall come." Where? To
God's house.

> "And I will fill this temple with glory," says the LORD of hosts.
> "The silver is Mine, and the gold is Mine," says the LORD of
> hosts. "The glory of this latter temple [the Church] shall be
> greater than the former," says the LORD of hosts. "And in this
> place I will give peace," says the LORD of hosts.
>
> Haggai 2:7–9

Can you see the great purpose? While everything else crashes
and trembles and shakes all around us, while the darkness gets
deeper, while the perplexity of nations increases, kings and
their rulers are going to turn to the risen light of the Church
of Jesus Christ. They are going to bring their treasures into
the Church that the purpose of God for the close of this age
may be accomplished: "This gospel of the kingdom will be
preached in all the world as a witness to all the nations, and
then the end will come" (Matthew 24:14).

The preaching of this Gospel of the Kingdom, the full
Gospel of Jesus—as Savior, Healer, Deliverer, Baptizer—is
going to be preached in all the world to all nations. Then
shall the end come.

Now listen: Let's be sensible. God says, "The silver is Mine,
and the gold is Mine." If the devil has money, he stole it.
Whom does it belong to? God. And He never gave the devil
any legitimate right to that money. God's people apologize
for having money. It is the world that should apologize, not
God's people. We are entitled to it.

"The silver is Mine, and the gold is Mine." "The glory of this latter temple shall be greater than the [glory of the] former." In other words, God says, "Bring Me the silver and the gold into My house and you will see what I will do." The Gospel of the Kingdom must be preached to complete the Church of Jesus Christ. For it must come from all kingdoms and nations and peoples and tribes and languages (see Revelation 7:9). The Gospel has to be preached in all the world—not in a watered-down human version, but in a demonstration of the power of the Holy Spirit such as Paul preached. Then shall the end come.

What is your part and mine? It is to rule in His Kingdom as priests, devoted to prayer and dedicated to filling His house with His glory.

God gave me a vision of what He planned for me two weeks after my being saved. I did not know it was a vision, I did not know what visions were, but it was very real. At that time it was like a distant mountain peak. There were tremendous areas of territory between me and that peak but I started out on the journey toward it.

Many times there were storms, clouds came down, the peak was obscured. Not only once, but several times I began to deviate from the pathway. Always in the mercy of God the clouds were dispelled, the sun came out and once again illuminated that peak. As I was going in a wrong direction, I corrected my direction and began to head for the peak again. That is, more than anything else, what has kept me in the pathway of God's will. It is having a vision, having something that I am working toward, something that I know God wants me to fulfill in my life.

I think I could say at this stage of my life, having been a Christian for many decades, this is the main motivation, the thing that dominates my thinking. I think I understand the words of Paul when he said, "That I may finish my race with joy, and the ministry which I received from the Lord Jesus" (Acts 20:24).

In my mind's eye I see that peak and I say, prayerfully, "By the grace of God, I will not stop until I reach it."

Will you join me?

This is my prayer for you. May you bring the Lord glory. May His Kingdom be established through your prayers. May you find your place in the Body of Christ, knowing God's will and defeating the enemy. May you and all you have be used to establish a royal priesthood welcoming God's Kingdom to the earth. And may you know the joy of answered prayer.

SUBJECT INDEX

SCRIPTURE INDEX

215

Derek Prince (1915–2003) was born in India of British parents. Educated as a scholar of Greek and Latin at Eton College and Cambridge University, England, he held a Fellowship in Ancient and Modern Philosophy at King's College. He also studied several modern languages, including Hebrew and Aramaic, at Cambridge University and the Hebrew University in Jerusalem.

While serving with the British army in World War II, he began to study the Bible and experienced a life-changing encounter with Jesus Christ. Out of this encounter he formed two conclusions: first, that Jesus Christ is alive; and second, that the Bible is a true, relevant and up-to-date book. These conclusions altered the whole course of his life, which he then devoted to studying and teaching the Bible.

Derek's main gift of explaining the Bible and its teaching in a clear and simple way has helped build a foundation of faith in millions of lives. His nondenominational, nonsectarian approach has made his teaching equally relevant and helpful to people from all racial and religious backgrounds.

He is the author of over 50 books, 600 audio teachings and 140 video teachings, many of which have been translated and published in more than 60 languages. His daily radio broadcast, *Derek Prince Legacy Radio*, is translated into Arabic, Chinese (Amoy, Cantonese, Mandarin, Shanghaiese, Swatow), Croatian, German, Malagasy, Mongolian, Russian,

Samoan, Spanish and Tongan. The radio program continues to touch lives around the world.

Derek Prince Ministries persists in reaching out to believers worldwide with Derek's teachings, fulfilling the mandate to keep on "until Jesus comes." This is effected through international offices in Australia, Canada, China, France, Germany, the Netherlands, New Zealand, Norway, Russia, South Africa, Switzerland, the United Kingdom and the United States.

For current information about these and other worldwide locations, visit www.derekprince.com.